CAMBRIDGE LIBRARY COLLECTION

Books of enduring scholarly value

Travel and Exploration in Asia

This collection of travel narratives, mainly from the nineteenth century, records the impressions of Europeans who visited China, Japan, South and South-East Asia. Some came as missionaries, others as members of trade or diplomatic missions, or as colonial administrators. Some were straightforward tourists, and one or two arrived as prisoners or shipwrecked sailors. Such accounts of travellers' experiences in exotic locations were eagerly received by European readers.

Travels in Kamtschatka

Jean-Baptiste-Barthélemy de Lesseps (1766–1834), a French diplomat, served as an interpreter on La Pérouse's voyage around the world, which sailed from Brest in 1785. In 1787, on the eastern coast of the Kamchatka peninsula, he was tasked with an overland mission to get reports back to France as La Pérouse proceeded to Australia. This two-volume work, reissued here in its English translation of 1790, is a compelling account of the one-year journey from Russia to France, and a tale of endurance and resourcefulness in the face of forbidding conditions. More than a mere journal, it also relates the author's observations on the way of life in Kamtchatka, its institutions and trade. Rich in detail, the work will appeal to historians and readers with an interest in transcontinental adventure. Volume 1 covers his journey from Petropavlovsk-Kamchatsky to the north-eastern extremity of the Sea of Okhotsk.

Cambridge University Press has long been a pioneer in the reissuing of out-of-print titles from its own backlist, producing digital reprints of books that are still sought after by scholars and students but could not be reprinted economically using traditional technology. The Cambridge Library Collection extends this activity to a wider range of books which are still of importance to researchers and professionals, either for the source material they contain, or as landmarks in the history of their academic discipline.

Drawing from the world-renowned collections in the Cambridge University Library and other partner libraries, and guided by the advice of experts in each subject area, Cambridge University Press is using state-of-the-art scanning machines in its own Printing House to capture the content of each book selected for inclusion. The files are processed to give a consistently clear, crisp image, and the books finished to the high quality standard for which the Press is recognised around the world. The latest print-on-demand technology ensures that the books will remain available indefinitely, and that orders for single or multiple copies can quickly be supplied.

The Cambridge Library Collection brings back to life books of enduring scholarly value (including out-of-copyright works originally issued by other publishers) across a wide range of disciplines in the humanities and social sciences and in science and technology.

Travels in Kamtschatka

During the Years 1787 and 1788

VOLUME 1

JEAN-BAPTISTE-BARTHÉLEMY DE LESSEPS

CAMBRIDGE
UNIVERSITY PRESS

University Printing House, Cambridge, CB2 8BS, United Kingdom

Published in the United States of America by Cambridge University Press, New York

Cambridge University Press is part of the University of Cambridge.
It furthers the University's mission by disseminating knowledge in the pursuit of
education, learning and research at the highest international levels of excellence.

www.cambridge.org
Information on this title: www.cambridge.org/9781108062824

© in this compilation Cambridge University Press 2013

This edition first published 1790
This digitally printed version 2013

ISBN 978-1-108-06282-4 Paperback

TRAVELS

IN

KAMTSCHATKA,

DURING THE YEARS 1787 AND 1788.

TRANSLATED FROM THE FRENCH OF

M. DE LESSEPS, CONSUL OF FRANCE,

AND

INTERPRETER TO THE COUNT DE LA PEROUSE, NOW
ENGAGED IN A VOYAGE ROUND THE WORLD, BY
COMMAND OF HIS MOST CHRISTIAN MAJESTY.

IN TWO VOLUMES.

VOLUME I.

L O N D O N:

PRINTED FOR J. JOHNSON, ST. PAUL'S CHURCH-YARD.
1790.

PREFACE.

M̲Y work is merely a journal of my travels. Why fhould I take any fteps to prepoffefs the judgment of my reader? Shall I not have more claim to his indulgence when I have affured him, that it was not originally my intention to write a book? Will not my account be the more interefting, when it is known, that my fole inducement to employ my pen was the neceffity I found of filling up my leifure moments, and that my vanity extended no farther than to give my friends a faithful journal of the difficulties I had to encounter, and the obfervations I made on my road? It is evident I wrote by inter-

vals,

vals, negligently or with care, as circumftances permitted, or as the impreffions
made by the objeɛts around me were more
or lefs forcible

Confcious of my own inexperience, I
thought it a duty I owed myfelf to let flip
no opportunity of acquiring information,
as if I had fotefeen, that I fhould be called
to account for the time I had fpent, and
the knowledge which I had it in my power
to obtain : but perhaps the fcrupulous ex-
aɛtnefs to which I confined myfelf, entailed
on my narration a want of elegance and
variety.

The events which relate perfonally to
myfelf are fo conneɛted with the fubjeɛt of
my remarks, that I have taken no care to
fupprefs them. I may therefore, not un-
defervedly, be reproached with having
fpoken

fpoken too much of myfelf: but this is the prevailing fin of travellers of my age.

Befides this, I am ready to accufe myfelf of frequent repetitions, which would have been avoided by a more experienced pen. On certain fubjects, particularly in refpect of travels, it is fcarcely poffible to avoid an uniformity of ftyle. To paint the fame objects, we muft employ the fame colours; hence fimilar expreffions are continually re-curring.

With refpect to the pronunciation of the Ruffian, Kamtfchadale, and other foreign words, I fhall obferve, that all the letters are to be articulated diftinctly. I have thought it advifeable, even in the vocabulary, to reject thofe confonants, the confufed affemblage of which difcourages the reader, and is not always neceffary. The *kh* is to be pronounced as the *ch* of the

A 3   Germans,

Germans, or the *j* of the Spaniards, and the *cb* as in the French. The finals *oi* and *in*, are to be pronounced, the former as an improper·diphthong (*oï*) and the latter in the Englifh, not in the French manner.

The delay of publifhing this journal renders fome excufe neceffary. Unquef-tionably I might have given it to the world fooner, and it was my duty to have done it ; but my gratitude bad me wait the re-turn of the count de la Péroufe. What is my journey, faid I to myfelf? To the pub-lic, it is only an appendage to the important expedition of that gentleman ; to myfelf, it is an honourable proof of his confidence: I had a double‚ motive to fubmit my ac-count to his infpection. My own intereft alfo prefcribed this to me. How happy fhould I have been, if, permitting me to publifh my travels as a fupplement to his, he had deigned to render me an affociate of

his

his fame ! This, I confefs, was the fole end
of my ambition ; the fole caufe of my delay.

How cruel for me, after a year of impatient expectation, to fee the wifhed for
period ftill more diftant! Not a day has
paffed fince my arrival, on which my
wifhes have not recalled the Aftrolabe and
Bouffole. How often, traverfing in imagination the feas they had to crofs, have I
fought to trace their progrefs, to follow
then from port to port, to calculate their
delays, and to meafure all the windings of
their courfe !

When at the moment of our feparation
in Kamtfchatka, the officers of our veffels
forrowfully embraced me as loft, who would
have faid, that I fhould firft revifit my native country ; that many of them would
never fee it more; and that in a little time
I fhould fhed tears over their fate !

A 4   Scarcely,

Scarcely, in effect, had I time to congratulate myfelf on the fuccefs of my miffion,
and the embraces of my family, when the
report of our misfortunes in the Archipe-
lago of navigators arrived, to fill my heart
with forrow and afflicton. The vifcount
de Langle, that brave and loyal feaman, the
friend, the companion of our commander;
a man whom I loved and refpected as my
father, is no more! My pen refufes to
trace his unfortunate end, but my gratitude indulges itfelf in repeating, that the
remembrance of his virtues and his kindnefs to me, will live eternally in my bofom.

Reader, who ever thou art, pardon this
involuntary effufion of my grief. Hadft
thou known him whom I lament, thou
wouldft mingle thy tears with mine: like
me thou wouldft pray to Heaven, that, for
our confolation, and for the glory of France,
the commander of the expedition, and thofe

of

of our brave Argonauts, whom it has preferved, may foon return. Ah! if whilft I
write, a favourable gale fhould fill their fails,
and impel them towards our fhores!—May
this prayer of my heart be heard! May the
day on which thefe volumes are publifhed,
be that of their arrival! In the excefs of
my joy, my felf-love would find the higheft
gratification.

CONTENTS

CONTENTS TO VOL. I.

Mode

Oftrog

Koriacs

Diftreffing

TRAVELS

TRAVELS

IN

KAMTSCHATKA, &c.

I HAVE fcarcely completed my twenty-
fifth year, and am arrived at the moft me-
morable æra of my life. However long, or
however happy may be my future career,
I doubt whether it will ever be my fate to
be employed in fo glorious an expedition
as that in which two French frigates, the
Bouffole, and the Aftrolabe, are at this moment engaged ; the firft commanded by
count de la Peroufe, chief of the expedition,
and the fecond by vifcount de Langle *.

The

* If my pen were equal to the fubject, what admirable
things might I relate of thefe celebrated men, formed to

The report of this voyage round the
world, created too general and lively an intereſt, for direct news of theſe illuſtrious
navigators, reclaimed by their country and
by all Europe from the ſeas they traverſe,
not to be expected with as much impatience as curioſity.

How flattering is it to my heart, after
having obtained from count de la Perouſe
the advantage of accompanying him for
more than two years, to be farther indebted
to him for the honour of conveying his diſpatches over land into France ! The more
I reflect upon this additional proof of his
confidence, the more I feel what ſuch an
embaſſy requires, and how far I am de-
ficient ; and I can only attribute his preference, to the neceſſity of chooſing for this

conduct a grand enterpriſe with the utmoſt harmony ? But
their exploits, and the public eſteem, have long placed them
above my praiſes.

journey,

journey, a perfon who had refided in Ruffia,
and could fpeak its language.

On the 6 September 1787, the king's
frigates entered the port of Avatfcha, or
Saint Peter and Saint Paul *, at the fouthern
extremity of the peninfula of Kamtfchatka.
The 29, I was ordered to quit the Aftrolabe ; and the fame day count de la Peroufe
gave me his difpatches and inftructions.
His regard for me would not permit him to
confine his cares to the moft fatisfactory arrangements for the fafety and convenience
of my journey; he went farther, and gave
me the affectionate counfels of a father,
which will never be obliterated from my
heart. Vifcount de Langle had the goodnefs to join his alfo, which proved equally
beneficial to me.

Let me be permitted in this place to pay

* Called by the Ruffians Petropavlosfkaia-gaven.

my juft tribute of gratitude to the faithful companion of the dangers and the glory of count de la Peroufe, and his rival in every other court, as well as that of France, for having acted towards me, upon all occafions, as a counfellor, a friend, and a father.

In the evening I was to take my leave of the commander and his worthy colleague. Judge what I fuffered, when I conducted them back to the boats that waited for them. I was incapable of fpeaking, or of quitting them; they embraced me in turns, and my tears too plainly told them the fituation of my mind. The officers who were on fhore, received alfo my adieux: they were affected, offered prayers to heaven for my fafety, and gave me every confolation and fuccour that their friendfhip could dictate. My regret at leaving them cannot be defcribed; I was torn from their arms, and found myfelf in thofe of

colonel

colonel Kafloff-Ougrenin, governor general
of Okotfk and Kamtfchatka, to whom count
de la Peroufe had recommended me, more
as his fon, than an officer charged with his
difpatches.

At this moment commenced my obliga-
tions to the Ruffian governor. I knew not
then all the fweetnefs of his character, inceffantly difpofed to acts of kindnefs, and
which I have fince had fo many reafons to
admire *. He treated my feelings with the
utmoft addrefs. I faw the tear of fympathy
in his eye upon the departure of the boats,
which we followed as far as our fight would
permit ; and in conducting me to his houfe,

* After loading with civilities every individual engaged
in the expedition, he was farther defirous of fupplying the
frigates with provifions. Notwithftanding the difficulty of
procuring oxen in this country, he furnifhed feven at his
own expence, and could be prevailed upon by no entreaties
to accept any equivalent, but regretted that he was not able
to procure a greater number.

he

he fpared no pains to divert me from my
melancholy reflections. To conceive the
frightful void which my mind experienced
at this moment, it is neceffary to be in my
fituation, and left alone in thefe fcarcely
difcovered regions, four thoufand leagues
from my native land : without calculating
this enormous diftance, the dreary afpect
of the country fufficiently prognofticated
what I fhould have to fuffer during my long
and perilous route; but the reception which
I met with from the inhabitants, and the
civilities of M. Kafloff and the other Ruffian officers, made me by degrees lefs fenfible to the departure of my countrymen.

It took place on the morning of 30 September. They fat fail with a wind that
carried them out of fight in a few hours,
and continued favourable for feveral days.
It will readily be believed, that I did not
fee them depart without offering the moft
fincere

fincere wifhes for all my friends on board;
the laft fad homage of my gratitude and
attachment.

Count de la Peroufe had recommended
diligence to me, but enjoined me, at the
fame time, upon no pretext to quit M.
Kaflof; an injunction that was perfectly
agreeable to my inclinations. The governor had promifed to conduct me as far as
Okotfk, which was the place of his refidence,
and to which it was neceffary that he fhould
repair immediately. I had already felt the
happinefs of being placed in fuch good
hands, and I made no fcruple of furrender-
ing myfelf implicity to his direction.

His intention was to go as far as Bolcheretfk, and there wait till we could avail
ourfelves of fledges, which would greatly
facilitate our journey to Okotfk. The feafon was too far advanced for us to rifk an

attempt

attempt by land, and the paſſage by ſea was not leſs dangerous ; beſides there was no veſſel either in the port of Saint Peter and Saint Paul, or of Bolcheretſk *.

M. Kofloff had his affairs to ſettle, which, with the preparations for our departure, detained us ſix days longer, and afforded me time to ſatisfy myſelf that the frigates were not likely to return. I embraced this opportunity of commencing my obſerva-tions, and making minutes of every thing about me. I attended particularly to the bay of Avatcha, and the port of Saint Peter and Saint Paul, in order to give a juſt idea of them.

This bay has been minutely deſcribed by captain Cook, and we found his account to be accurate. It has ſince undergone ſome

---

* The navigation is ſufficiently ſafe in ſummer, and is the only mode of travelling that is adopted.

alter-

alterations; which, it is faid, are to be followed by many others; particularly as to
the port of Saint Peter and Saint Paul. It
is poffible indeed, that the very next fhip
which fhall arrive, expecting to find only
five or fix houfes, may be furprifed with the
fight of an entire town, built of wood, but
tolerably fortified.

Such at leaft is the projected plan, which,
as I learned indirectly, is to be afcribed to
M. Kafloff, whofe views are equally great,
and conducive to the fervice of his miftrefs.
The execution of this plan will contribute
not a little to increafe the celebrity of the
port, already made famous by the foreign
veffels which have touched there, as well as
by its favourable fituation for commerce *.

To

* According to the accounts of the earlieft navigators, it
is the moft commodious port in this part of Afia, and ought
to be the general depôt for the commerce of the country.
This would be fo much the more advantageous, as the veffels
which frequent the other ports, commonly confider themfelves

To underftand the nature, and eftimate
the utility of this project, nothing more is
neceffary

felves as fortunate if they efcape fhipwreck; and for this
reafon the Emprefs has exprefsly prohibited all navigation
after the 26th of September.

I learned a circumftance at the fame time, which con-
firms what I have faid, and feems to have occafioned the
firft idea of thefe improvements.

An Englifh fhip, belonging to M. Lanz, a merchant of
Macao, came to anchor in the port of Saint Peter and Saint
Paul, in the year 1786. Captain Peters, who commanded
the veffel, made propofals of commerce to the Ruffians, of
which the following are the particulars. By a treaty which
he had entered into with a Ruffian merchant, named Schelikhoff, he engaged to carry on a commerce with this part
of the ftates of the Emprefs, and demanded goods to the
amount of eighty thoufand roubles. Thefe goods would
probably have confifted of furs, which the Englifh expected
to find a market for in China, from whence they would
have brought back in exchange ftuffs and other articles ufeful to the Ruffians. Schelikhoff repaired immediately to
Saint Peterfburg, to folicit the confent of his fovereign,
which he obtained; but while was endeavouring to fulfil
the conditions of his engagement, he learned that the Englifh veffel had been loft upon the coaft of Copper Ifland (*Ile
de Cuivre*) in its return to Kamtfchatka from the north-
weft part of America, where it was probable it had failed,

in

neceffary than to have an idea of the extent
and form of the bay of Avatfcha, and the
port in queftion. We have already many
accurate defcriptions, which are in the
hands of every one. I fhall therefore confine myfelf to what may tend to illuftrate
the views of M. Kafloff.

The port of St. Peter and St. Paul, is
known to be fituated at the north of the
entrance of the bay, and clofed in at the
fouth by a very narrow neck of land, upon
which the oftrog*, or village of Kamtfchatka

in order to begin its cargo, which it expected to complete
at the port of Saint Peter and Saint Paul. Two only of
the crew were known to have been faved, a Portuguefe and
a Bengal negro, who paffed the winter at Copper Ifland,
from whence a Ruffian veffel conveyed them to Nijenei-
Kamtfchatka. We joined them at Bolcheretfk, and it was
M. Kafloff's intention to fend them next feafon to Peterfburg.

* The word *oftrog* properly fignifies a conftruction furrounded with pallifadoes. Its etymology may be derived, I
imagine, from the entrenchments haftily conftructed by the
Ruffians

fchatka is built. Upon an eminence to the eaft, at the moft interior point of the bay, is the houfe of the governor*, with whom M. Kafloff refided during his ftay. Near this houfe, almoft in the fame line, is that of a corporal of the garrifon, and a little higher inclining to the north, that of the ferjeant, who, next to the governor, are the only perfons at all diftinguifhed in this fettlement, if indeed it deferves the name of fettlement. Oppofite to the entrance of the port, on the declivity of the eminence, from which a lake of confiderable extent is feen, are the ruins of the hofpital mentioned in captain Cooke's voyage †. Below thefe,

Ruffians to protect them from the incurfions of the natives, who, doubtlefs, did not paffively fuffer their country to be invaded. The appellation of oftrog is now given to almoft all the villages in this country.

* His name was Khabaroff, and he had the rank of a *preporchik*, or enfign.

† At a little diftance from this fpot was buried, at the foot of a tree, the body of captain Clerke. The infcription
which

thefe, and nearer the fhore, is a building which ferves as a magazine to the garrifon, and which is conftantly guarded by a centinel. Such was the ftate in which we found the port of St. Peter and St. Paul.

By the propofed augmentation, it will evidently become an interefting place. The entrance was to be clofed, or at leaft flanked by fortifications, which were to ferve at the fame time as a defence, on this fide, to the projeted town, which was chiefly to

which the Englifh placed upon his tomb, was on wood, and liable to be effaced. Count de la Peroufe, defirous that the name of this navigator fhould be immortalifed, without having any thing to fear from the injuries of the weather, fubftituted inftead of it an infcription on copper.

It is needlefs to mention, that he enquired at the fame time where the famous French aftronomer, from the ifland of Croyere, had been buried. He entreated M. Kafloff to order a tomb to be erefted, and an epitaph, which he left engraved on copper, to be placed on it, containing an elogy, and the circumftances of the death of our countryman. I faw his intentions carried into execution after the departure of the French frigates.

be

be built upon the fite of the old hofpital;
that is, between the port and the lake. A
battery alfo was to be erected upon the
neck of land which feparates the bay from
the lake, in order to protect the other part
of the town. In fhort, by this plan, the
entrance of the bay would be defended
by a fufficiently ftrong battery upon the
leaft elevated point of the left coaft; and
veffels entering the bay could not efcape
the cannon, becaufe of the breakers on the
right. There is at prefent upon the point
of a rock, a battery of fix or eight cannon,
lately erected to falute our frigates.

I need not add, that the augmentation of
the garrifon forms a part of the plan, which
confifts only at prefent of forty foldiers, or
Coffacs. Their mode of living and their
drefs are fimilar to the Kamtfchadales, except that in time of fervice they have a
fabre, firelock, and cartouch box; in other
refpects

refpects they are not diftinguifhable from
the indigenes, but by their features and
idiom.

With refpect to the Kamtfchadale village, which forms a confiderable part of
the place, and is fituated, as I have already
faid, upon the narrow projection of land
which clofes in the entrance of the port,
it is at prefent compofed of from thirty
to forty habitations, including winter and
fummer ones, called *ifbas* and *balagans*; and
the number of inhabitants, taking in the
garrifon, does not exceed a hundred, men,
women and children. The intention is to
increafe them to upwards of four hundred.

To thefe details refpecting the port of St.
Peter and St. Paul, and its deftined improvements, I fhall add a few remarks upon
the nature of the foil, the climate, and the
rivers.

rivers. The banks of the bay of Avatſcha
are rendered difficult of acceſs by high
mountains, of which ſome are covered with
wood, and others have volcanos*. The valleys preſent a vegetation that aſtoniſhed me.
The graſs was nearly of the height of a
man; and the rural flowers, ſuch as the
wild roſes and others that are interſperſed
with them, diffuſe far and wide a moſt
grateful ſmell.

The rains are in general heavy during
ſpring and autumn, and blaſts of wind are
frequent in autumn and winter. The latter is ſometimes rainy; but notwithſtanding its length, they aſſured me that its ſe-
verity is not very extreme, at leaſt in this

* There is a volcano about fifteen or twenty werſts from
the port, which the naturaliſts who accompanied count
de la Perouſe viſited, and which will be mentioned in his
voyage. The inhabitants informed me that ſmoak often
iſſued from it, but that an eruption, which uſed to be frequent, had not happened for many years.

ſouthern

fouthern part of Kamtfchatka*. The fnow
begins to appear on the ground in October,
and the thaw does not take place till April
or May ; but even in July it is feen to fall
upon the fummit of high mountains, and
particularly volcanos. The fummer is
tolerably fine; the ftrongeft heats fcarcely
laft beyond the folftice. Thunder is feldom
heard, and is never productive of injury.

* The exceffive cold of which the Englifh complain,
may not be without example ; and I pretend not to contra-
dict them. But as a proof that the rigour of the climate is
not fo very piercing, the inhabitants, whom they reprefent
as not daring to come out of their fubterraneous dwellings,
or *yourts*, during the whole winter, for fear of being frozen,
no longer conftruct any of thefe caves in this fouthern part
of the peninfula, as I fhall have occafion to obferve elfewhere. I acknowledge, however, that the cold which I
experienced during my abode there, and which may be
compared to that of the winter of 1779, appeared to me
very fimilar to what is felt at Saint Peterfburg. What the
Englifh muft have had reafon to fuppofe extraordinary, are
the dreadful hurricanes, which bring on fuch thick and
heavy ftorms of fnow, that it is not poffible either to venture
out, or to advance, if we are on a journey. I experienced
this more than once, as will be feen in the fequel.

VOL. I.   C   Such

Such is the temperature of almoſt all this part of the peninſula.

Two rivers pour their waters into the bay of Avatſcha; that from which the bay is named, and the Paratounka. They both abound with fiſh, and every ſpecies of water fowl, but theſe are ſo wild, that it is not poſſible to approach within fifty yards of them. The navigation of theſe rivers is impraƈticable after the 26 November, becauſe they are always frozen at this time; and in the depth of winter the bay itſelf is covered with ſheets of ice, which are kept there by the wind blowing from the ſea ; but they are completely difpelled as ſoon as it blows from the land. The port of St. Peter and St. Paul is commonly ſhut up by the ice in the month of January.

I ſhould doubtlefs ſay ſomething in this place of the manners and cuſtoms of the Kamt-

Kamtfchadales, of their houfes, or rather huts, which they call *ifbas* or *balagans*; but I muft defer this till my arrival at Bolche-retfk, where I expect to have more leifure, and a better opportunity of defcribing them minutely.

We departed from the port of Saint Peter and Saint Paul the 7 October. Our com-pany confifted of Meffrs. Kafloff, Schmaleff*, Vorokhoff†, Ivafchkin ‡, myfelf, and the fuite

---

* M. Schmaleff is infpector general for the Kamtfcha-dales, or, as it is called in Ruffia, *capitan-ifpravnik* for the department of Kamtfchatka; he is the fame perfon whom the Englifh had fo much reafon to praife, and the good offices he rendered us intitle him equally to our efteem.

† Secretary to the governor; he is employed in civil affairs, and ranks as an officer.

‡ M. Ivafchkin is the unfortunate gentleman mentioned by the Englifh, and who merits in every refpect the eulo-gium beftowed on him. The mere recital of his misfor-tunes is fufficient to excite the compaffion of every reader; but it is neceffary to have feen and obferved him, to

judge

fuite of the governor, amounting to four
ferjeants, and an equal number of foldiers.
The

judge of the extreme intereſt which his unhappy lot is calculated to inſpire.

He was not twenty years of age, when the empreſs
Elizabeth made him ſerjeant of her guard of Preobrajenſkoi.
He already enjoyed a certain credit at court, and the free
acceſs to the ſovereign, which his office gave him, opened
the moſt brilliant career to his ambition ; when all at once
he ſaw himſelf not merely diſgraced and deprived of all his
flattering hopes, but treated as the greateſt criminal ; he
was *knouted*, which is the ſevereſt and moſt degrading
puniſhment practiſed in Ruſſia, had his noſe ſlit, and was
baniſhed for life to Kamtſchatka.

The Engliſh have told us what he ſuffered for more than
twenty years, from the rigour with which he was treated ;
he was denied even the firſt neceſſaries of life, and muſt infallibly have periſhed of hunger and miſery, or fallen a prey
to deſpair, if the force of his mind and the ſtrength of his
conſtitution had not ſupported him. The neceſſity of providing for his own ſubſiſtence, compelled him, not without
diſguſt, to naturalize himſelf with the Kamtſchadales, and
to adopt entirely their mode of living ; he is clothed like them,
and by means of hunting and fiſhing is enabled to procure,
not merely a ſufficiency for his wants, but a ſuperfluity, from
the ſale of which he obtains ſome little couveniencies that
ſeem to ſweeten his miſerable exiſtence. He reſides at Verck-
-neï

The commanding officer of the port, probably out of refpect to M. Kafloff, his
fuperior,

nei-Kamtfchatka, or Upper Kamtfchatka. The Ruffians
are ignorant of the caufe of fo fevere a punifhment; they
are difpofed to attribute it to a mifunderftanding, or fome
indifcreet words, for they know not how to fuppofe him
capable of a crime. It feems as if a change of fentiment
had taken place refpecting the pretended enormity of his
offence, a propofal having been lately made of changing the
place of his banifhment, and removing him to Yakoutfk, a
town that offers a variety of refources, both for profit and
pleafure. But this unfortunate being, who is from fixty to
fixty-five years of age, has refufed to avail himfelf of this
permiffion, not wifhing, as he faid, to make a fhow of the
hideous marks of his difhonour, and to blufh a fecond time
at the dreadful punifhment he has undergone. He preferred the continuing to live with the Kamtfchadales, having
but one defire left, that of paffing the few remaining days
of life with thofe who know his integrity, and of carrying
with him to his grave the general friendfhip and efteem, to
which he is fo juftly intitled.

The accounts given by the Englifh, excited in count de
la Peroufe a defire to fee this unfortunate man, who infpired
him from the firft moment with the moft lively pity. He
received him on board his fhip, and at his table. The
count's humanity was not confined to compaffionating his
miferies; he fought every means of foftening them, by
leaving him whatever was calculated to remind him of our

C 3   abode

fuperior, joined our little troop, and we embarked upon *baidars**, in order to crofs the
bay and reach Paratounka, where we were
to be fupplied with horfes to proceed on
our route.

In five or fix hours we arrived at this
oftrog, where the prieft †, or rector of the
diftrict refides, and whofe church alfo is in
this place ‡. His houfe ferved us for a lodg-

ing,

abode there, and prove to him that the Englifh are not the
only foreigners interefted in his forrowful lot.

* *Baidars* are boats fomewhat fimilar to European ones,
except that the fides are made of planks from four to fix
inches wide, and faftened together with withies or cords;
and that they are caulked with mofs. The baidars are the
only veffels made ufe of to fail to the Kurilles iflands;
they are commonly rowed, but will admit of a fail.

† His name is *Feodor Verefchaguin*; he fucceeded his
eldeft brother Romanoff Verefchaguin, who fhewed fo
many civilities to captain Clerke, and whom I afterwards
found at Bolcheretfk.

‡ His predeceffor had informed the Englifh that this parifh was to be immediately transferred to the oftrog of St.

Peter

ing, and we were treated with the utmoft
hofpitality ; but we had fcarcely entered
when the rain fell in fuch abundance, that
we were obliged to ftay longer than we
wifhed.

I eagerly embraced this fhort interval to
defcribe fome of the objects which I had
deferred till my arrival at Bolcheretfk,
where, perhaps, I may find others that will
not be lefs interefting.

The oftrog of Paratounka is fituated by
the fide of a river of that name, about two
leagues from its mouth *. This village is
fcarcely

Peter and St. Paul ; but this cannot take place till the projected improvements refpecting the port are carried into
execution. We cannot help obferving, that the Englifh
have omitted to mention that there was formerly a church
at St. Peter and St. Paul's, and that its fituation is known
by means of a fort of tomb which formed a part of it.

* This river empties itfelf, as I have already faid, into
the bay of Avatfcha. The fhoals, which are commonly

dry

fcarcely more populous than that of St.
Peter and St. Paul. The fmall pox has,
in this place particularly, made dreadful ravages. The number of balagans and ifbas
feemed to be very nearly the fame as at
Petropavlofska*.

The Kamtfchadales lodge in the firft during fummer, and retreat to the laft in
winter. As it is thought defirable that,

dry at low water, render its entrance impracticable; it is
even difficult at high water.

* As I ftood to examine the Kamtfchadale houfes, I
frequently imagined to myfelf the difdainful furprife that
our French Sybarites would exprefs at the fight, fome of
whom are fo proud of their vaft hotels, and others fo jea-
lous of their little neat and decorated apartments, where the
art of arrangement fcarcely falls fhort of the refined luxury
of fuperb furniture. I conceived them to exclaim—How
can human beings live in thefe miferable huts! A Kamtfchadale however, is by no means unhappy in thefe cabins,
whofe architecture feem to lead us back to the firft age of
the world; he lives there with his family in tranquillity;
he enjoys at leaft the happinefs of knowing few privations,
and of having therefore lefs wants, and has no objects of
envious comparifon before his eyes.

they

they fhould be brought gradually to refemble the Ruffian peafants, they are prohibited, in this fouthern part of Kamtfchatka, from conftructing any more *yourts,*
or fubterraneous habitations; thefe are all
deftroyed at prefent *, a few veftiges only
remain of them, filled up within, and appearing externally like the roofs of our ice-
houfes.

The balagans are elevated above the
ground upon a number of pofts, placed at
equal diftances, and about twelve or thirteen feet high.   This rough fort of colon-
nade fupports in the air a platform made of
rafters, joined to one another, and overfpread
with clay : this platform ferves as a floor to
the whole building, which confifts of a roof
in the fhape of a cone, covered with a kind

---

* I met with fome afterwards in the northern part,
which I took care to examine, and have defcribed in their
proper place.

of

of thatch, or dried grafs, placed upon long
poles faftened together at the top, and bear-
ing upon the rafters. This is at once the
firft and laft ftory ; it forms the whole apartment, or rather chamber: an opening in
the roof ferves inftead of a chimney to let
out the fmoke, when a fire is lighted to
drefs their victuals ; this cookery is per-
formed in the middle of the room, where
they eat and fleep pell-mell together without the leaft difguft or fcruple. In thefe
apartments, windows are out of the queftion ; there is merely a door, fo low and
narrow, that it will fcarcely fuffice to admit the light. The ftair-cafe is worthy of
the reft of the building ; it confifts of a
beam, or rather a tree jagged in a flovenly
manner, one end of which refts on the
ground, and the other is raifed to the height
of the floor. It is placed at the angle of
the door, upon a level, with a kind of open
gallery that is erected before it. This tree
retains

retains its roundnefs, and prefents on one
fide fomething like fteps, but they are fo
incommodious that I was more than once
in danger of breaking my neck. In reality,
whenever this vile ladder turns under the
feet of thofe who are not accuftomed to
it, it is impoffible to preferve an equilibrium ; a fall muft be the confequence,
more or lefs dangerous, in proportion to
the height. When they wifh perfons to be
informed that there is nobody at home,
they merely turn the ftair-cafe, with the
fteps inward.

Motives of convenience may have fug-
gefted to thefe people the idea of building
fuch ftrange dwellings, which their mode
of living renders neceffary and commodious. Their principal food being dried fifh,
which is alfo the nourifhment of their
dogs, it is neceffary, in order to dry their
fifh, and other provifions, that they fhould
have

have a place fheltered from the heat of the
fun, and at the fame time perfectly expofed to
the air. Under the collonnades or ruftic por-
ticos, which form the lower part of their
balagans, they find this convenience ; and
there they hang their fifh, either to the
ceiling or to the fides, that it may be out
of the reach of the voracioufnefs of their
dogs. The Kamtfchadales make ufe of
dogs * to draw their fledges ; the beft, that
is the moft vicious, have no other kennel
than what the portico of the balagans affords them, to the pofts of which they are
tied. Such are the advantages refulting
from the fingular mode of conftructing
the balagans, or fummer habitations of the
Kamtfchadales.

Thofe of winter are lefs fingular ; and if

* As I fhall foon be obliged to adopt this mode of travelling, I fhall defer my defcription of the dogs till that
period.

equally

equally large, would exactly refemble the
habitations of the Ruffian peafants. Thefe
have been fo often defcribed, that it is univerfally known how they are conftructed and
arranged. The ifbas are built of wood;
that is to fay, the walls are formed by placing long trees horizontally upon one another, and filling up the interftices with
clay. The roof flants like our thatched
houfes, and is covered with coarfe grafs, or
rufhes, and frequently with planks. The
interior part is divided into two rooms, with
a ftove placed fo as to warm them both, and
which ferves at the fame time as a fire-
place for their cookery. On two fides of
the largeft room, wide benches are fixed,
and fometimes a forry couch made of
planks, and covered with bears fkin. This
is the bed of the chief of the family : and
the women, who in this country are the
flaves of their hufbands, and perform all

the

the moſt laborious offices, think themſelves
happy to be allowed to ſleep in it.

Beſides theſe benches and the bed, there
is alſo a table, and a great number of images
of different ſaints, with which the Kamtſchadales are as emulous of furniſhing their
chambers, as the majority of our celebrated
connoiſſeurs are of diſplaying their magni-
ficent paintings.

The windows, as may be ſuppoſed, are
neither large or high. The panes are
made of the ſkins of ſalmon, or the blad-
ders of various animals, or the gullets of ſea
wolves prepared, and ſometimes of leaves
of talc ; but this is rare, and implies a ſort
of opulence. The fiſh ſkins are ſo ſcraped
and dreſſed that they become tranſparent,
and admit a feeble light to the room * ;

* They produce an effect ſomewhat ſimilar to the oiled
paper in the windows of our manufactories.

but

but objects cannot be feen through them.
The leaves of talc are more clear, and approach nearer to glafs ; in the mean time
they are not fufficiently tranfparent for
perfons without to fee what is going on
within : this is manifeftly no inconvenience
to fuch low houfes.

Every oftrog is prefided by a chief, called
toyon. This kind of magiftrate is chofen
from among the natives of the country,
by a plurality of voices. The Ruffians
have preferved to them this priviledge,
but the election muft be approved by the
jurifdiction of the province. This toyon
is merely a peafant, like thofe whom he
judges and governs; he has no mark of
diftinction, and performs the fame labours
as his fubordinates. His office is chiefly to
watch over the police, and infpect the execution of the orders of government. Under him is another Kamtfchadale, chofen

ı   by

by the toyon himfelf, to affift him in the
exercife of his functions, or fupply his
place. This vice-toyon is called *yefaoul*, a
Coffac title adopted by the Kamtfchadales
fince the arrival of the Coffacs in their
peninfula, and which fignifies fecond chief
of their band or clan. It is neceffary to
add, that when the conduct of thefe chiefs
is confidered as corrupt, or excites the
complaints of their inferiors, the Ruffian
officers prefiding over them, or the other
tribunals eftablifhed by government, dif-
mifs them immediately from their functions, and nominate others more agreeable
to the Kamtfchadales, with whom the right
of election ftill remains.

The rain continuing, we were unable
to proceed on our journey ; but my curiofity led me to embrace a fhort interval
that offered in the courfe of the day, to
walk

walk out into the oftrog, and vifit its environs.

I went firft to the church, which I found
to be built of wood, and ornamented in the
tafte of thofe of the Ruffian villages. I
obferved the arms of captain Clerke, painted by Mr. Webber, and the Englifh infcription upon the death of this worthy
fucceffor of captain Cook ; it pointed out the
place of his burial at Saint Peter and Saint
Paul's.

During the ftay of the French frigates
in this port, I had been at Paratounka,
in a hunting excurfion, with vifcount de
Langle. As we returned, he fpoke of
many interefting objects he had obferved
in the church, and which had entirely efcaped my attention. They were, as
far as I can remember, various offerings
depofited there, he faid, by fome an-

cient navigators, who had been fhipwrecked. It was my full intention to examine them upon my fecond vifit to this
oftrog ; but whether it efcaped my recollec-
tion, or that my refearch was too precipitate, from the fhort time that I had to make
it, certain it is that I did not difcover them.

The village is furrounded with a wood ;
I traverfed it by proceeding along the river,
and perceived at length a vaft plain which
extends to the north and the eaft as far as
the mountains of Petropavlofska. This
chain is terminated at the fouth and weft
by another, of which the mountain of Paratounka forms a part, and which is about
five or fix werfts* from the oftrog of that
name. Upon the banks of the rivers that
wind in this plain, there are frequent traces

* A werft is exactly ten hundred yards. This feems
not accurately to agree with the fcale of werfts in the
map. We leave it to the reader to follow which authority he pleafes. T.

of

of bears, who are attracted by the fish with
which thefe rivers abound. The inhabitants affured me, that fifteen or eighteen
were frequently feen together upon thefe
banks, and that whenever they hunted
them, they were fure to bring back one or
two, at leaft, in the fpace of twenty-four
hours. I fhall foon have occafion to fpeak
of their chace, and their weapons.

We quitted Paratounka and refumed our
journey; twenty horfes fufficed for ourfelves and our baggage, which was not confiderable, M. Kafloff having taken the precaution of fending a great part of it by
water, as far as the oftrog of Koriaki. The
river Avatfcha has no tide, and is not navigable farther than this oftrog; and not at
all indeed, except by fmall boats, called
batts. The baidirs only ferve to crofs the
bay of Avatfcha, and can proceed no farther than the mouth of the river, where

their

their lading is put into thefe batts, which,
from the fhallownefs and rapidity of the
water, are pufhed forward with poles. It
was in this manner our effects arrived at
Koriaki.

As to ourfelves, having croffed the river
Paratounka at a fhallow, and winded along
feveral of its branches, we left it for a way
that was woody and lefs level, but which
afforded us better travelling; it was almoft
entirely in valleys, and we had only two
mountains to climb. Our horfes, notwithftanding their burthens, advanced very
brifkly. We had no reafon to complain of
the weather for a fingle moment; it was fo
fair, that I began to think the rigour of
the climate had been exaggerated; but
fhortly after, experience too well convinced
me of its truth, and in the fequel of my
journey, I had every reafon to accuftom myfelf to the moft piercing frofts, too happy
                                    when

when in the midft of ice and fnow, that I
had not to contend with the violence of
whirlwinds and tempefts.

We were about fix or feven hours in
going from Paratounka to Koriaki, which,
as far as I could judge, is from thirty-
eight to forty werfts. Scarcely arrived, we
were obliged to take refuge in the houfe of
the *toyon*, to fhelter ourfelves from the rain ;
he ceded his ifba to M. Kafloff, and we
fpent the night there.

The oftrog of Koriaki is fituated in the
midft of a coppice wood, and upon the border of the river Avatfcha, which becomes
very narrow in this part. Five or fix ifbas,
and twice, or at moft three times the number of balagans, make up this village, which
is fimilar to that of Paratounka, except that
it is lefs, and has no parifh church. I obferved in general that oftrogs of fo little

D 3   con-

confideration were not provided with a
church.

The next day we mounted our horfes
and took the way to Natchikin, another
oftrog in the Bolcheretfk route. We were
to ftop a few days in the neighbourhood for
the fake of the baths, which M. Kafloff had
conftructed at his own expence, for the benefit and pleafure of the inhabitants, upon
the hots fprings that are found there, and
which I fhall prefently defcribe. The way
from Koriaki to Natchikin is tolerably commodious, and we croffed without difficulty
all the little ftreams that fall from the
mountains, at the foot of which we paffed.
About three-fourths of the way we met the
Bolchaia-reka*; from the fite of its greateft
breadth, which in this place is about ten or
twelve yards, it appears to wind to a confiderable extent to the north eaft; we jour-

* A Ruffian name which fignifies, *large river.*

neyed

neyed on its bank for fome time, till we
came to a little mountain, which we were
obliged to pafs over in order to reach the
village. A heavy rain which came on as
we left Koriaki, ceafed a few minutes after;
but the wind having changed to the north-
weft, the heavens became obfcured, and we
had abundance of fnow; we were about
two-thirds of our way, and it continued till
our arrival. I remarked that the fnow already covered the mountains, even fuch as
were loweft, upon which it defcribed an
equal line at a certain elevation, but that
below them no traces of it were yet perceptible. We forded the Bolchaia-reka,
and found on the other fide the oftrog of
Natchikin, where I counted fix or feven
ifbas and twenty balagans, fimilar to what
I had feen before. We made no ftay there,
M. Kafloff thinking it proper to haften immediately to the baths, to which I was in-

D 4 clined

clined as much from curiofity as from neceffity.

The fnow had penetrated through my
clothes, and in croffing the river, which was
deep, I had made my legs and feet wet. I
longed therefore to be able to change my
drefs, but when we came to the baths our
baggage was not arrived. We propofed dry-
ing ourfelves by walking about the environs, and obferving the interefting objects
which I expected to find there. I was
charmed with every thing 1 faw, but the
dampnefs of the place, added to that of our
clothes, gave us fuch a chillinefs that we
quickly put an end to our walk. Upon
our return we had a new fource of regret
and impatience. Unable either to dry ourfelves or change our drefs, our equipage not
being arrived, to complete our misfortune,
the place to which we had retired was the
dampeft we could have chofen, and though

it

it feemed fufficiently fheltered, the wind penetrated on every fide. M. Kafloff had recourfe to the bath, which quickly reftored
him; but not daring to follow his example, I was obliged to wait the arrival of
our baggage. The damp had penetrated to
fuch a degree that I fhivered during the
whole night.

The next day I made a trial of thefe
baths, and can fay that none ever afforded
me fo much pleafure or fo much benefit.
But before I proceed, I muft defcribe the
fource of thefe hot waters, and the building conftructed for bathing.

They are two werfts to the north of the
oftrog, and about a hundred yards from the
bank of the Bolchaia-reka, which it is neceffary to crofs a fecond time in order to arrive
at the baths, on account of the elbow which
the river defcribes below the village. A thick
and

and continual vapour afcends from thefe
waters, which fall in a rapid cafcade from a
rather fteep declivity, three hundred yards
from the place where the baths are erected.
In their fall, which is in a direction eaft and
weft, they form a fmall ftream of a foot and
half deep, and fix or feven feet wide. At a
little diftance from the Bolchaia-reka, this
ftream is met by another, with which it pours
itfelf into this river. At their conflux, which
is about eight or nine hundred yards from
the fource, the water is fo hot that it is not
poffible to keep the hand in it for half a
minute.

M. Kafloff has been careful to erect his
building on the moft convenient fpot, and
where the temperature of the water is moft
moderate. It is conftructed of wood, in the
middle of a ftream, and is in the proportion of fixteen feet long by eight wide. It
is divided into two apartments, each of fix
or

or feven feet fquare, and as many high:
the one which is nearest to the fide of
the fpring, and under which the water is
confequently warmer, is appropriated for
bathing; the other ferves for a dreffing-
room; and for this purpofe there are wide
benches above the level of the water; in
the middle alfo a certain fpace is left to
wafh if we be difpofed. There is one
circumftance that renders thefe baths very
agreeable, the warmth of the water com-
municates itfelf fufficiently to the dreffing-
room to prevent us from catching cold;
and it penetrates the body to fuch a degree, as to be felt even for the fpace of an
hour or two after we have left the bath.

We lodged near thefe baths in a kind of
barns, covered with thatch, and whofe
timber work confifted of the trunks and
branches of trees. We occupied two,
which had been built on purpofe for us,
and

and in fo fhort a time, that I knew not how
to credit the report; but I had foon the
conviction of my own eyes. That which
was to the fouth of the ftream, having been
found too fmall and too damp, M. Kafloff
ordered another of fix or eight yards extent, to be built on the oppofite fide, where
the foil was lefs fwampy. It was the bufinefs of a day; in the evening it was finifh-
ed, though an additional ftaircafe had been
cut out to form a communication between
the barn and the bathing houfe, whofe door
was to the north.

Our habitations being infupportable during the night, on account of the cold, M.
Kafloff refolved to quit them, four days
after our arrival. We returned to the village to fhelter ourfelves with the toyon;
but the attraction of the baths led us back
every day, oftener twice than once, and we
fcarcely ever came away without bathing.

The

The various conftruétions which M.
Kafloff ordered for the greater convenience
of his eftablifhment, detained us two days
longer. Animated by a love of virtue and
humanity, he enjoyed the pleafure of having
procured thefe falutary and pleafant baths
for his poor Kamtfchadales. The uninformed ftate of their minds, or perhaps their
indolence, would, without his fuccour, have
deprived them of this benefit, notwithftanding their extreme confidence in thefe
hot fprings for the cure of a variety of difeafes*. This made M. Kafloff defirous of
afcertaining the properties of thefe waters;
we agreed to analyfe them, by means of a
procefs which had been given him for this
purpofe. But before I fpeak of the refult
of our experiments, it is neceffary to tranf-
cribe the procefs, in order the better to
trace the mode we adopted.

* Formerly they dared not approach thefe fprings, or
any volcano, from the idea that they were the abode of evil
fpirits.

Water

" Water in.general may contain,

" 1. Fixed air; in that cafe it has a
" fharp and fourifh tafte, like lemonade,
" without fugar.

" 2. Iron or copper; and then it has
" an aftringent and difagreeable tafte, like
" ink.

" 3. Sulphur, or fulphurous vapours; and
" then it has a very naufeous tafte, like
" a ftale and rotten egg.

" 4. Vitriolic, or marine, or alkaline falt.

" 5. Earth."

Fixed Air.

" To afcertain the fixed air, the tafte is
" partly fufficient; but pour into the water
" fome tincture of turnfol, and the water
" will

" will become more or lefs red, in propor-
" tion to the quantity of fixed air it con-
" tains."

Iron.

" The iron may be known by means of
" the galnut and phlogifticated alkali; the
" galnut put into feruginous water, will
" change its colour to purple, or violet, or
" black; and the phlogifticated alkali will
" produce immediately Pruffian blue."

Copper.

" Copper may be afcertained by means
" of the phlogifticated alkali or volatile al-
" kali; the firft turns the water to a brown
" red, and the fecond to a blue. The laft
" mode is the fureft, becaufe the volatile
" alkali precipitates copper only, and not
" iron."

Sulphur.

Sulphur.

" Sulphur and fulphurous vapours may
" be known by pouring, 1. nitrous acid into
" the water; if a yellowifh or whitifh fedi-
" ment be formed by it, there is fulphur, and
" at the fame time a fulphurous odour will
" be exhaled and evaporate. 2. By pouring
" fome drops of a folution of corrofive fubli-
" mate; if it occafion a white fediment, the
" water contains only vapours of liver of
" fulphur; and if the fediment be black, the
" water contains fulphur only.

Vitriolic Salt.

" Water may contain vitriolic falts; that
" is falts refulting from the combination of
" the vitriolic acid with calcareous earth,
" iron, copper, or with an alkali. The vi-
" triolic acid may be afcertained by pouring
" fome drops of a folution of heavy earth;
" for then a fandy fediment will be formed,
" which will fettle flowly at the bottom of
" the veffel.

Marine

Marine Salt.

" Water may contain marine falt, which
" may be afcertained by pouring into it fome
" drops of a folution of filver ; a white fedi-
" ment will immediately be formed of the
" confiftency of curdled milk, which will at
" laft turn to a dark violet colour.

Fixed Alkali.

" Water may contain fixed alkali, which
" may be afcertained by pouring into it
" fome drops of a folution of corrofive fub-
" limate ; when a reddifh fediment will be
" formed.

Calcareous Earth.

" Water may contain calcareous earth
" and magnefia. Some drops of acid of
" fugar poured into the water, will preci-
" pitate the calcareous earth in whitifh
" clouds, which will at length fubfide and

" afford

" afford a white fediment. A few drops of
" a folution of corrofive fublimate, will pro-
" duce a reddifh fediment, but very gra-
" dually, if the water contain magnefia.

" Note. To make thefe experiments with
" readinefs and certainty, the water to be
" analyfed fhould be reduced one half by
" boiling it, except in the cafe of the fixed
" air, which would evaporate in the boiling."

Having thoroughly ftudied the procefs,
we began our experiments. The three firft
producing no effect, we concluded that the
water contained neither fixed air, iron, nor
copper; but upon the mixture of the nitrous acid, mentioned for the fourth experiment, we perceived a light fubftance fettle
upon the furface, of a whitifh colour, and
extending but a little way, which led us to
believe that the quantity of fulphur, or

of

of fulphurous vapours, muft be infinitely
fmall.

The fifth experiment proved that the
water contained vitriolic falts, or at leaft
vitriolic acid mixed with calcareous earth.
We afcertained the exiftence of this acid,
by pouring fome drops of a folution of
heavy earth into the water, which became
white and nebulous, and the fediment that
flowly fettled at the bottom of the veffel
appeared whitifh and in very fine grains.

We had no folution of filver for the fixth
experiment, in order to afcertain whether
the water contained marine falt.

The feventh proved that it had no fixed
alkali.

By the eighth experiment, we found that
the water contained a great quantity of
cal-

calcareous earth, but no magnefia. Having
poured fome drops of acid of fugar, we obferved the calcareous earth precipitate to the
bottom of the veffel in clouds and a powder
of a whitifh colour ; we mixed afterwards
fome folution of corrofive fublimate to find
the magnefia ; but the fediment, inftead
of becoming red, preferved the fame colour as before ; a proof that the water contained no magnefia.

We made ufe of this water for tea and
for our common drink.   It was not till after
three or four days that we found it contained fome faline particles.

M. Kafloff boiled alfo fome of the water
taken at the fpring, till it became totally
evaporated ; the whitifh and very falt earth
or powder which remained at the bottom of
the veffel, as well as the effect it produced
on

on us, proved that this water contained nitrous falts.

We remarked alfo that the ftones taken
out of this ftream were covered with a calcareous fubftance tolerably thick, and of an
undulated appearance, which, when mixed
with the vitriolic and nitrous acid, produced
fymptoms of effervefcence. We examined
others taken from what appeared to be the
fountain head of the waters, and where
they have the greateft degree of heat; we
found them covered with a ftratum of a
kind of metal, if I may fo call a hard and
compact envelopement of the colour of refined copper, but the quality of which we
could not afcertain; we found alfo fome of
this metal, which appeared like the heads
of pins; but no acid could diffolve it. Upon
breaking thefe ftones, we difcovered the infide to be very foft and mixed with gravel,

with

with which I had obferved thefe ftreams
to abound.

I ought to add here, that we difcovered
upon the border of the ftream, and in a little moving fwamp that was near it, a gum,
or fingular *fucus* *, that was glutinous, but
did not adhere to the ground.

Such are the obfervations which I made
upon thefe hot waters, by affifting M. Kafloff
in his experiments and enquiries. I dare
not flatter myfelf with having given the refult of our operations in a fatisfactory manner; forgetfulnefs, or want of information
upon the fubject, may have led me into
errors; I can only fay that I have exerted all my attention and care to be accurate; but acknowledge at the fame time,

---

* M. Kafloff gave fome of this gum to one of the na-
turalifts of our expedition, the abbé Mongés, while the
frigates were at Saint Peter and Saint Paul.

that

that if there be defects, they are afcribable
to me.

During our ftay at thefe baths and at the
oftrog of Natchikin, our horfes had brought,
at different times, the effects which we had
left at Koriaki, and we began to make preparations for our departure. In this interval I had an opportunity of feeing a fable
taken alive; the method was very fingular,
and may give fome idea of the manner of
hunting thefe animals.

At fome diftance from the baths, M. Kafloff remarked a numerous flight of ravens,
who all hovered over the fame fpot, fkim-
ming continually along the ground. The
regular direction of their flight led us to
fufpect that fome prey attracted them.
Thefe birds were in reality purfuing a fable.
We perceived it upon a birch-tree, furrounded by another flight of ravens, and

E 4   we

we had immediately a fimilar defire of
taking it. The quickeft and fureft way
would doubtlefs have been to have fhot it ;
but our guns were at the village, and it
was impoffible to borrow one of the perfons
who accompanied us, or indeed in the whole
neighbourhood. A Kamtfchadale happily
drew us from our embaraffment, by under-
taking to catch the fable. He adopted the
following method. He afked us for a cord ;
we had none to give him but that which faftened our horfes. While he was making a
running knot, fome dogs, trained to this
chace, had furrounded the tree : the animal,
intent upon watching them, either from fear,
or natural ftupidity, did not ftir ; and contented himfelf with ftretching out his neck,
when the cord was prefented to him. His
head was twice in the noofe, but the knot
flipped. At length, the fable having
thrown himfelf upon the ground, the dogs
flew to feize him ; but he prefently freed
him-

himfelf, and with his claws and teeth laid
hold of the nofe of one of the dogs, who
had no reafon to be pleafed with his reception. As we were defirous of taking
the animal alive, we kept back the dogs;
the fable quitted immediately his hold, and
ran up a tree, where, for the third time, the
noofe, which had been tied anew, was prefented to him; it was not till the fourth
attempt that the Kamtfchadale fucceeded *.
I could not have imagined that an animal,
who has fo much the appearance of cunning, would have permitted himfelf to be
caught in fo ftupid a manner, and would
himfelf have placed his head in the fnare
that was held up to him. This eafy mode
of catching fables, is a confiderable refource
to the Kamtfchadales, who are obliged to

* M. Kafloff, who prefided in this chace, had the politenefs to make me a prefent of this fable, called in this country *fobol*, and promifed to add it to another, that I might
bring a couple with me to France.

pay their tribute in fkins of thefe animals, as I fhall explain hereafter *.

Two phenomena in the heavens were obferved at the north-weft, during the nights of the 13 and 14. From the defcription that was given of them, we judged that they were auroræ boreales, and we lamented that we were not informed time enough to fee them. The weather had been tolerably fair during our ftay at the baths ; but the weftern part of the fky had been almoft conftantly charged with very thick clouds. The wind varied from weft to north-weft, and gave us now and then a fhower of fnow, which did not yet acquire confiftency, notwithftanding the frofts which we experienced every night.

Our departure was fixed for the 17 Octo-

* Thefe fkins are not only a confiderable branch of commerce, but ferve as a fpecies of money with the Kamt-fchadales,

ber,

ber, and the 16 was fpent in the hurry and
buftle which the laft preparations generally
occafion. The reft of our route, as far as
Bolcheretfk, was to be upon the Bolchaia-
reka. Ten fmall boats, which properly
fpeaking, appeared to be merely trees
fcooped out in the fhape of canoes, two and
two lafhed together, ferved as five floats
for the conveyance of ourfelves and part of
our effects. We were obliged to leave the
greater part at Natchikin, on account of
the impoffibility of loading thefe floats with
the whole, and there were no means of in-
creafing them. We had already collected
all the canoes that were in the village, and
even fome of our ten had been brought
from the oftrog of Apatchin, to which we
were going.

The 17, at break of day, we embarked
upon thefe floats. Four Kamtfchadales, by
means of long poles, conducted our rafts.

But

But they were frequently obliged to place
themfelves in the water, in order to haul
them along ; the depth of the river in fome
places being no more than one or two feet,
and in others lefs than fix inches. Prefently one of our floats received an injury ;
it was precifely that which was freighted
with our baggage, and we were obliged to
unlade every thing upon the bank, in order
to refit it. We waited not, but preferred
leaving it behind, in order to proceed on
our route. At noon another accident, much
more deplorable for men whofe appetites
began to be clamorous, occafioned us a further delay. The float in which our cookery
was embarked, funk all at once before our
eyes. It will be fuppofed we did not fee
the lofs which threatened us, with indiffer-
enc ; we were eager to fave the wreck of
our provifions ; and for fear of a greater
misfortune, we wifely refolved to dine before we proceeded any farther. Our din-
                                          ner

ner tended gradually to difpel our fears,
and gave us courage to difcharge the water
which over-loaded our boats, and to refume our voyage. We had not advanced a
werft, before we met two boats coming
to our affiftance from Apatchin. We fent
them to the fuccour of the damaged float,
and to fupply the place of the boats which
were unfit for fervice. As we continued
to advance at the head of our embarkations,
we at laft entirely loft fight of them; but
we met with nothing difaftrous till the
evening.

I obferved that the Bolchaia-reka, in the
windings which it continually made, ran
nearly in the direction of eaft-north-eaft
and weft-fouth-weft. Its current is very
rapid; it appeared to me to flow at the
rate of five knots an hour; in the mean-
time the ftones and the fhoals which we
met with every inftant, obftructed our paffage

fage to fuch a degree, as to render the labour of our conductors truly painful. They
avoided them with aftonifhing addrefs, but
as we approached nearer the mouth of the
river, I obferved with pleafure that it became wider and more navigable. I was
equally furprifed to fee it divide into I know
not how many branches, which united
again, after having watered a variety of
little iflands, of which fome are covered
with wood. The trees are every where
very fmall and very bufhy ; we met with a
confiderable number growing here and
there in the very river itfelf, which increafe
ftill farther the difficulty of the navigation,
and prove the careleffnefs, I may fay the
floth, of thefe people. It never occurs to
them to root out thefe trees, and thus open
a more eafy paffage.

Different fpecies of water-fowl, fuch as
ducks, plovers, goëlands, divers, and others,
divert

divert themſelves in this river, the ſurface
of which is ſometimes covered by them;
but it is difficult to approach near enough
to ſhoot them. Game does not appear to
be ſo common. But for the tracks of the
bears, and the half-devoured fiſh, which
continually preſented themſelves to our
view, I ſhould have believed that they
had impoſed upon me, or at leaſt that they
had exaggerated, in telling me of the multitude of theſe animals with which the
country abounds; we could perceive none;
but we ſaw a great number of black eagles,
and others that had white wings; magpies,
ravens, ſome partridges, and an ermine
walking by the ſide of the river.

Upon the approach of night, M. Kaſloff
rightly judged that it would be more pru-
dent to ſtop, than to continue our route,
with the apprehenſion of encountering obſtacles ſimilar to what had already impeded

our

our navigation. How were we to furmount
them ? we were unacquainted with the
river ; and in the obfcurity of the night,
the leaft accident might prove fatal to us.
Thefe confiderations determined us to leave
our boats, and to pafs the night on the
right-hand bank of the river, at the entrance of a wood, and near the place where
captain King and his party halted *. A
good fire warmed and dried our whole company. M. Kafloff had taken the precaution to place in his float the accoutrements
of a tent ; and while we were pitching it,
which was done in a moment, we had the
fatisfaction to fee two of our floats arrive,
which had not been able to keep up with
us. The pleafure which this reunion afforded us, the fatigue of the day, the convenience of the tent, and our beds, which
we had fortunately brought with us, all

See Cook's Voyage, vol. III. p. 208.

contributed

contributed to make us pafs a moft com-
fortable night.

The next day we fitted ourfelves out
early and without difficulty. We arrived
in four hours at Apatchin, but our floats
could not come up as far as the village,
on account of the fhallownefs of the water. We landed about four hundred yards
from the oftrog, and atchieved this fhort
diftance on foot.

This village did not appear to me fo
confiderable as the preceding ones, that is,
it contained perhaps three or four habitations lefs. It is fituated in a fmall plain,
watered by a branch of the Bolchaïa-reka ;
and on the fide oppofite to the oftrog is an
extent of wood, which I conceived might
be an ifland formed by the different branches
of this river.

I learned

I learned by the way, that the oſtrog
of Apatchin, as well as that of Natchikin, had not been always where they are at
preſent. It is within a few years only that
the inhabitants, attracted without doubt by
the ſituation, or the hope of better and
more commodious fiſhing, removed their
houſes to this place. The diſtance of the
new oſtrog from the former one is, as I
was told, about four or five werſts.

Apatchin afforded nothing intereſting.
I left it to join our floats, which had paſſed
the ſhallows, and were waiting for us three
werſts from the oſtrog, at the ſpot where
the branch of Bolchaïa-reka, after having
made a circuit round the village, returns
again to its channel. The farther we advanced, the deeper and more rapid we
found it ; ſo that nothing impeded our
courſe the whole way to Bolcheretſk, where
we arrived at ſeven o'clock in the evening,

accom-

accompanied by one only of our floats, the
reft not having kept pace with us.

We were no fooner landed, than the governor conducted me to his houfe, where
he had the civility to give me a lodging,
which I occupied during the whole time of
my ftay at Bolcheretfk. He not only procured me all the conveniences and pleafures
that were in his power, but furnifhed me
with all the information which might contribute to my advantage, and which his
office permitted him to give. His politenefs often anticipated my defires and my
queftions; and he contrived to ftimulate my
curiofity, by prefenting to it every thing
which he thought was calculated to intereft me. It was with this view he propofed,
almoft immediately upon our arrival, my
going with him to view the galliot from
Okotfk, that had been unfortunately juft

fhip-

fhipwrecked at a little diftance from Bolcheretfk.

We had learned fomething of this melancholy news in our journey. It was faid
that the bad weather, which the galliot
had encountered at its arrival, obliged it to
come to anchor at the diftance of a league
from the coaft; but finding that it ftill
drove, the pilot faw no other means of
faving the cargo than by running the veffel
aground upon the coaft; accordingly he
cut the cables, and the fhip was dafhed to
pieces.

Upon the firft intelligence of this event,
the inhabitants of Bolcheretfk flocked together to haften to the fuccour of the veffel,
and to fave at leaft the provifions with which
it was freighted. Immediately upon our
arrival, M. Kafloff had given all the orders
which

which appeared to him to be neceffary;
but not fatisfied with this, he would go
himfelf to fee them carried into execution.
He invited me to accompany him, which I
accepted with cheerfulnefs, promifing myfelf much pleafure from having an opportunity of viewing the mouth of the Bolchaïa-reka, and the harbour which is formed
by it.

We fet off at eleven o'clock in the morning, upon two floats, of which one, that
which carried us, was formed of three canoes. Our conductors made ufe of oars and
fometimes of their poles, which frequently
in difficult and fhallow paffages, enabled
them to refift the impetuofity of the current, by keeping back the float, which would
otherwife have been carried along with rapidity and infallibly overturned.

The Biftraïa, another very rapid river,
and

and larger than the Bolchaïa-reka, joins it
to the weft, about the diftance of half a
werft from Bolcheretfk. It lofes its name
at the conflux, and takes that of the Bolchaïa-reka, which is rendered very confiderable by this addition, and empties itfelf
into the fea at the diftance of thirty werfts.

We landed at feven o'clock in the evening at a little hamlet called *Tchekafki*. Two
ifbas, two balagans, and a yourt almoft in
ruins, were all the habitations I could perceive. There was alfo a wretched ware-
houfe, made of wood, to which they give
the name of magazine, becaufe it belongs
to the crown, and firft receives the fupplies with which the galliots from Okotfk*
are freighted. The hamlet was built as a
guard to this magazine, We paffed the

* When thefe galliots are obliged to winter here, they
harbour in the mouth of a narrow and deep river, which
pours itfelf into the Bolchaïa-reka, about fifty yards from
the hamlet, higher up.

night

night in one of the ifbas, refolving to repair
early in the morning to the wreck.

At break of day we embarked upon our
floats. It was low water; we coafted along
a dry and very extenfive fand bank, at the
left of the Bolchaïa-reka, as we advanced towards the fea, and which leaves to the north
a paffage of only eight or ten fathoms
wide, and two and a half deep. The wind,
which blew frefh from the north-weft,
fuddenly agitated the river, and we dared
not rifk ourfelves in the channel. Our boats
alfo were fo fmall, that a fingle wave half
filled them; two men were conftantly employed in throwing out the water, and were
fcarcely able to effect it. We advanced
therefore as far as we could along this
bank.

At length we perceived the maft of the
galliot above a neck of low land that ex-
          F 4   tended

tended to the fouth. It appeared to be
about two werfts from us, fouth of the entrance of the Bolchaïa-reka. At the point
of land juft mentioned, we difcovered the
light houfe, and the cot of the perfons appointed to guard the wreck: unfortunately
we could only fee all this at a diftance. The
direction of the river, from the place where
it empties itfelf into the fea, appeared to
me to be north-weft, and its opening to be
half a werft wide. The light-houfe is on
the left coaft, and on the right is the con-
tinuation of the low land, which the fea
overflows in tempeftuous weather, and which
extends almoft as far as the hamlet of Tchekafki. The diftance of the hamlet from the
mouth of the river is from fix to eight
werfts. The nearer we approach the entrance, the more rapid is the current.

It was not poffible to purfue our voyage;
the wind became ftronger, and the waves
increafed

increafed every moment. It would have
been the height of imprudence to quit the
fand bank, and crofs, in fuch foul weather
and fuch feeble boats, two werfts of deep
water, which is the width of the bay formed by the mouth of the river. The governor, who had already met with fome proofs
of my little knowledge of navigation, was
very anxious however to confult me upon
this occafion. My advice was to tack about,
and return to the hamlet where we had
flept; which was executed immediately.
We had great reafon to be pleafed with our
prudence; fcarcely were we arrived at
Tchekafki when the weather became terrible.

I confoled myfelf with the idea, that I
had at leaft obtained my end, which was to
fee the entrance of the Bolchaïa-reka. I
can affert with confidence, that the accefs
to it is very dangerous, and impracticable

to

to fhips of a hundred and fifty tons burthen. The Ruffian veffels are too frequently
fhipwrecked, not to open the eyes both of
navigators who may be tempted to vifit
this coaft, and of the nations who may
think of fending them.

The port, befides, affords no fhelter. The
low lands with which it is furrounded, are
no protection againft the winds which blow
from every quarter. The banks alfo which
the current of the river forms, are very
variable, and of courfe it is almoft impoffible to know with certainty the channel,
which muft neceffarily, from time to time,
change it direction as well as its depth.

We paffed the reft of the day at Tchekafki, being unable to proceed to the fhipwrecked veffel, or to return to Bolcheretfk.
The fky, inftead of clearing up, became
covered on all fides with ftill blacker and
thicker

thicker clouds. Soon after our arrival, a
dreadful tempeſt aroſe, and the Bolchaïa-
reka became agitated to an extreme violence, even ſo high up as our hamlet. Its
billows ſurpriſed me, becauſe of the little
extent and depth of the river in this place.
The point north-eaſt of its mouth, and the
low land, which this gale of wind extended,
formed but one breaker, over which the
waves rolled with a horrible noiſe. The
gale was not likely to abate, but I was on
ſhore, and thought myſelf able to brave it,
I took it into my head therefore, to go a
hunting in the environs of the hamlet. I
had ſcarcely advanced a few ſteps, when the
wind ſeized me, and I felt myſelf ſtagger;
my courage however did not fail me, and I
perſevered; but coming to a ſtream, which
it was neceſſary to croſs in a boat, I ran the
moſt imminent riſk, and returned immediately, well puniſhed for my petty pre-
ſumption. Theſe dreadful hurricanes being
                                        very

very common at this feafon, it is not be won-
dered at that fhipwrecks are fo frequent on
thefe coafts: the veffels are fo fmall as to
have but one maft; and, what is ftill worfe,
the failors who manage them, if report may
be credited, have too little fkill to be confided in.

The next day we refumed our journey,
and arrived at Bolcheretfk in the dufk of
the evening.

As I forfee that my ftay here will probably be long, from the neceffity of waiting till fledges can be ufed, I fhall proceed
with my defcriptions, and the recital of
what I have feen myfelf, or learned from
my converfations with the Ruffians and
Kamtfchadales. I fhall begin with the
town, or fort of Bolcheretfk, for fo it is
called, in Ruffia *(oftrog, or krepoft).*

It is fituated on the border of the Bol-
chaïa-

chaïa-reka, in a fmall ifland formed by different branches of this river, which divide
the town into three parts more or lefs inhabited. The moft diftant divifion, and which
is fartheft to the eaft, is a kind of fuburb
called *Paranchine*; it contains ten or twelve
ifbas. South eaft of Paranchine, is the middle divifion, where there is alfo a number
ifbas, and among others, a row of wooden
huts that ferve for fhops. Oppofite to thefe
is the guard-houfe, which is alfo the chancery, or court of juftice*; this houfe is
larger than the reft, and is always guarded
by a centinel. A fecond branch of the Bolchaïa-reka again feparates, by a very narrow ftream, this group of habitations, built
without order, and fcattered here and there,
from another at the north-weft, nearer the
river. The river in this part flows in the

* This guard-houfe is likewife ufed as a prifon, and
even as a fchool for children. The mafter of the fchool is
a Japanefe; he is fkilled in many languages, and is paid
by government for inftruhing the children of this country.

direction

direction of fouth-eaft and north-weft, and
paffes within fifty yards of the governor's
houfe. This houfe is eafily diftinguifhed
from the reft; it is higher, larger, and is
built like the wooden houfes of St. Peterfburg. Two hundred yards north-eaft of
this houfe, is the church; the conftruction
of which is fimple, and like that of the village churches in Ruffia. By the fide of
it is an erection of timber work, twenty
feet high, covered only with a roof, under
which three bells are fufpended. North-
weft of the governor's houfe, and feparated
from it by a meadow or marfh about three
hundred yards wide, is another group of
dwellings, confifting of twenty-five or thirty
ifbas, and fome balagans. There are in general very few of thefe latter habitations at
Bolcheretfk; the whole do not exceed ten;
the ifbas and wooden houfes, without including the eight fhops, the chancery, and
the governor's houfe, amount to fifty or
fixty.

From

From this minute defcription of the fort
of Bolcheretfk, it muft appear ftrange that
it retains fo inapplicable a name; for I can
affirm, that no traces are to be found of fortifications, nor does it appear that there has
ever been an intention of erecting any.
The ftate and fituation, both of the town
and its port, induce me to believe, that government have felt the innumerable dangers
and obftacles they would have to furmount,
if they were to attempt to render it more
flourifhing, and make it the general depôt
of commerce to the peninfula. Their views,
as I have already obferved, feem rather
turned to the port of Saint Peter and Saint
Paul, which for its proximity, fafety, and
eafy accefs, merits the preference.

There is a degree of civilization at Bolcheretfk, which I did not perceive at Petropavlofska. This fenfible approach to European manners, occafions a ftriking difference

rence between the two places. I ſhall endeavour to point out and account for this
as I proceed in my obſervations upon the
inhabitants of theſe oſtrogs; for my principal object ſhould be, to give details of
their employments, their cuſtoms, their
taſtes, their diverſions, their food, their un-
derſtandings, their character, their conſti-
tutions, and laſtly, the principles of government to which they are ſubjected.

The population of Bolcheretſk, including
men, women and children, amounts to between two and three hundred. Among
theſe inhabitants, reckoning the petty officers, there are ſixty or ſeventy Coſſacs, or
ſoldiers, who are employed in all labours
that relate to the ſervice of government*.
Each in his turn mounts guard; they clear
the ways; repair the bridges; unlade the

* Their pay is ſo inconſiderable, that the receipt of a
whole year would not ſuffice to maintain them for a ſingle
month, if they had not the reſource of a petty fraudulent
commerce, of which I ſhall preſently give an account.

prov"
}

provifions

provifions fent from Okotfk, and convey
them from the mouth of the Bolchaïa-reka
to Bolcheretfk. The reft of the inhabitants
are compofed of merchants and failors.

Thefe people, Ruffians and Coffacs, together with a mixed breed found among
them, carry on a clandeftine commerce,
fometimes in one article, and fometimes in
another; it varies as often as they fee any
reafon for changing it; but it is never with
a view of enriching themfelves by honeft
means. Their induftry is a continual kna-
vifhnefs; it is folely employed in cheating
the poor Kamtfchadales, whofe credulity
and infuperable propenfity to drunkennefs,
leave them entirely at the mercy of thefe
dangerous plunderers. Like our mountebanks, and other knaves of this kind, they
go from village to village to inveigle the
too filly natives: they propofe to fell them
brandy, which they artfully prefent to them

to tafte. It is almoft impoffible for a Kamtfchadale, male or female, to refufe this offer,
The firft effay is followed by many others;
prefently their heads become affected, they
are intoxicated, and the craft of the temp-
ters fucceed. No fooner are they arrived
to a ftate of inebriety, than thefe pilferers
know how to obtain from them the barter
of their moft valuable effects, that is, their
whole ftock of furs, frequently the fruit
of the labour of a whole feafon, which was
to enable them to pay their tribute to the
crown, and procure perhaps fubfiftance
for a whole family. But no confideration can ftop a Kamtfchadale drunkard;
every thing is forgotten, every thing is
facrificed to the gratification of his ap-
petite, and the momentary pleafure of
fwallowing a few glaffes of brandy*, re-
duces

* This is well known to be the ruling paffion of all the
people of the north; but I have had more than one occafion to obferve, that the Kamtfchadales are inferior in this
refpect

duces him to the utmoſt wretchedneſs.
Nor is it poſſible for the moſt painful experience to put them on their guard againſt
their own weakneſs, or the cunning perfidy
of theſe traders, who in their turn drink,

reſpect to none of them. The following ſtory, among
others, was told me, that I might be able to judge of the
rapacity of theſe vagabond traders, and the ſtupid prodiga-
lity of their dupes.

A Kamtſchadale had given a ſable for a glaſs of brandy.
Inflamed with a deſire of drinking another, he invited the
ſeller into his houſe. The merchant thanked him, but
ſaid he was in a hurry. The Kamtſchadale renewed
his ſolicitations, and propoſed a ſecond bargain : he prevailed.—" Come, another glaſs for this ſable, it is a finer
" one than the firſt.—No; I muſt keep the reſt of my
" brandy; I have promiſed to ſell it at ſuch a place, and I
" muſt be gone.—Stay a moment; here are two ſables.—
" 'Tis all in vain.—Well, come, I will add another.—
" Agreed, drink." Meanwhile the three ſables are ſeized,
and the hypocrite makes a freſh pretence to come away:
his hoſt redoubles his importunities to retain him, and demands a third glaſs : further refuſals and further offers : the
higher the chapman raiſes his price, the more the Kamtſchadale is prodigal of his furs. Who would have ſuppoſed that it would have ended in the ſacrifice of ſeven moſt
beautiful ſables for this laſt glaſs! they were all he had.

G 2

in

in like manner, all the profits of their knavery.

I fhall terminate the article of commerce by adding, that the perfons who deal moft in wholefale, are merely agents of the merchants of Totma, Vologda, Grand Uftiug, and different towns of Siberia, or the factors of other opulent traders, who extend even to this diftant country their commercial fpeculations.

All the wares and provifions, which neceffity obliges them to purchafe from the magazines, are fold exceffively dear, and at about ten times the current price at Mofcow. A *vedro* * of French brandy cofts eighty roubles †. The merchants are al-

* A Ruffian meafure containing from fifteen to twenty quarts.

† Eighteen pounds fterling, eftimating the rouble at four fhillings and fixpence.

lowed

lowed to traffic in this article; but the
brandy, diftilled from corn, which is brought
from Okotfk, and that produced by the
country, which is diftilled from the *flatkaïa-trava*, or fweet herb, are fold, upon
government account, at forty one roubles
ninety-fix kopecks* the vedro. They can
be fold only in the *kabacs*, or public houfes,
opened for that purpofe. At Okotfk, the
price of brandy diftilled from corn is no
more than eighteen roubles the vedro; fo
that the expence of freight is charged at
twenty-three roubles ninety-fix kopecks,
which appears exorbitant, and enables us
to form fome judgment of the accruing
profit.

The reft of the merchandize confifts of
nankins and other China ftuffs, together
with various commodities of Ruffian and
foreign manufacture, as ribands, handker-

* Nine pounds nine fhillings.

G 3   chiefs,

chiefs, ftockings, caps, fhoes, boots, and
other articles of European drefs, which may
be regarded as luxuries, compared with the
extreme fimplicity of apparel of the Kamtfchadales. Among the provifion imported,
there are fugar, tea, a fmall quantity of cof-
fee, fome wine, but very little, bifcuits, con-
fections, or dried fruits, as prunes, raifins,
&c. and laftly, candles, both wax and tallow,
powder, fhot, &c.

The fcarcity of all thefe articles in fo diftant a country, and the need, whether natural or artificial, which there is for them,
enable the merchants to fell them at whatever exorbitant price their voracity may
affix. In common, they are difpofed of almoft immediately upon their arrival. The
merchants keep fhops, each of them occu-
pying one of the huts oppofite the guard-
houfe; thefe fhops are open every day, except feaft days.

The

The inhabitants of Bolcheretſk differ not from the Kamtſcadales in their mode of living; they are leſs ſatisfied, however, with balagans, and their houſes are a little cleaner.

Their clothing is the ſame. The outer garment, which is called *parque*, is like a waggoner's frock, and is made of the ſkins of deer, or other animals, tanned on one ſide. They wear under this long breeches of ſimilar leather, and next the ſkin a very ſhort and tight ſhirt, either of nankin or cotton ſtuff; the women's are of ſilk, which is a luxury among them. Both ſexes wear boots; in ſummer, of goats or dogs ſkins tanned; and in winter, of the ſkins of ſea wolves, or the legs of rein deer*. The men conſtantly wear fur caps; in the mild ſeaſon they put on longer ſhirts of nankin,

* Articles of apparel made of the ſkins of rein deer are procured from the Koriacs.

or

or of ſkin without hair ; they are made like
the parque, and anſwer the ſame purpoſe,
that is, to be worn over their other garments.   Their gala dreſs, is a parque trim-
med with otter ſkins and velvet, or other
ſtuffs and furs equally dear.   The women
are clothed like the Ruſſian women, whoſe
mode of dreſs is too well known to need a
deſcription ; I ſhall therefore only obſerve,
that the exceſſive ſcarcity of every ſpecies of
ſtuff at Kamtſchatka, renders the toilet of
the women an object of very conſiderable
expence : they ſometimes adopt the dreſs of
the men.

The principal food of theſe people conſiſts, as I have already obſerved, in dried
fiſh.   The fiſh are procured by the men,
while the women are employed in domeſtic
occupations, or in gathering fruits and other
vegetables, which, next to the dried fiſh,
are the favourite proviſions of the Kamtfchadales

fchadales and Ruffians of this country.
When the women go out to make thefe harvefts for winter confumption, it is high holy-
day with them, and the anniverfary is celebrated by a riotous and intemperate joy, that
frequently gives rife to the moft extravagant
and indecent fcenes. They difperfe in crouds
through the country, finging and giving
themfelves up to all the abfurdities which
their imagination fuggefts; no confideration
of fear or modefty reftrains them. I cannot better defcribe their licentious frenzy
than by comparing it with the bacchanals
of the Pagans. Ill betide the man whom
chance conducts and delivers into their
hands! however refolute or however active
he may be, it is impoffible to evade the fate
that awaits him; and it is feldom that he
efcapes, without receiving a fevere flagel-
lation.

Their provifions are prepared nearly in
the

the following manner ; it will appear, from
the recital, that they cannot be accufed of
much delicacy. They are particularly careful to wafte no part of the fifh. As foon as
it is caught they tear out the gills, which
they immediately fuck with extreme gratification. By another refinement of fenfuality or gluttony, they cut off alfo at the
fame time fome flices of the fifh, which they
devour with equal avidity, covered as they
are with clots of blood. The fifh is then
gutted, and the entrails referved for their
dogs. The reft is prepared and dried;
when they eat it either boiled, roafted, or
broiled, but moft commonly raw.

The food which the epicures efteem moft,
and which appeared to me to be fingularly
difgufting, is a fpecies of falmon, called
tchaouitcha. As foon as it is caught, they
bury it in a hole ; and in this kind of larder
they leave it till it has had time to four, or,

properly

properly fpeaking, become perfectly pu-
trified. It is only in this ftate of corruption
that it attains the flavour moft pleafing to
the delicate palates of thefe people. In my
opinion the infectious odour that exhales
from this fifh, would fuffice to repulfe the
moft hungry being ; and yet a Kamtfchadale feeds voluptuoufly upon this rotten flefh. How fortunate does he confider
himfelf when the head falls to his lot! this
is deemed the moft delicious morfel, and is
commonly diftributed into many parts. I
frequently wifhed to overcome my averfion,
and tafte this fo highly valued food; but
my refolution was unequal to it ; and I was
not only unable to tafte it, but even to bring
it near my mouth ; every time I attempted,
the fetid exhalation which it emitted gave me
a naufea, and difgufted me infuperably.

The moft common fifh in Kamtfchatka
are trouts, and falmon of different fpecies;

fea

fea wolves are alfo eaten; the fat of this fifh
is very wholefome, and ferves them befide
for lamp oil.

Among the vegetables which are made
ufe of by the Kamtfchadales, the principal
are *farana* root, wild garlic, *flatkaïa-trava*,
or fweet herb, and other plants and fruits
nearly fimilar to what are found in Ruffia.

The *farana* is known to botanifts*. Its
fhape, its fize, and its colour have been
defcribed at large in the third voyage of
captain Cook. Its farinaceous root ferves
inftead of bread †. It is dried before it is

---

* By the name of *lilium flore atro rubente*.

† The Coffacs ufe rye alfo, which makes a fort of black
bread, like that of the Ruffian peafants. Government al-
lows them a certain quantity of rye flour, but it is infuffi-
cient, and they are obliged to procure more at their own
expence. Some of them lay it up in ftore in order to profit by its future fale.

ufed;

uſed; but it is wholeſome and nouriſhing
in whatever mode it may be prepared.

From the wild garlic* they make a harſh
and fermented beverage, which has a very
unpleaſant taſte; it is alſo uſed in various
ſauces; the Kamtſchadales are very fond of it.

The ſlatkaïa-trava, or ſweet herb, is plea-
ſant enough when it is freſh. This plant†
has alſo been minutely deſcribed by the
Engliſh. It is highly eſteemed by the natives, particularly the ſpirit diſtilled from
it. Soon after it is gathered, they ſlit it in
two, and ſcrape out the pith with a muſ-
cle-ſhell: they then dry it for winter, and

---

* It is called in Kamtſchatka, *tſcheremſcha.* Gmelin
denominates it: *allium foliis radicalibus petiolatis, floribus
umbellatis.* Vol. 1. p. 49.

† *Spondilium foliolis pinnatifidis.* See Linn. The juice
of the rind of this plant is ſo acrid, that it is impoſſible to
touch it without bliſtering the hand. In gathering it they
take care to wear gloves.

when

when they ufe it in their ragouts, it is previoufly boiled. Brandy is alfo diftilled from
this fweet herb, which, as I obferved before,
is fold on account of government: for this
purpofe the plant is purchafed of the
Kamtfchadales *.

There are three forts of inhabitants, the
natives or Kamtfchadales, the Ruffians and
Coffacs, and the defcendants from intermarriages.

The indigenes, that is, thofe whofe blood
is unmixed, are few in number; the fmall
pox has carried off three fourths of them,
and the few that are left are difperfed
through the different oftrogs of the peninfula; in Bolcheretfk it would be difficult to
find more than one or two.

* This brandy intoxicates much quicker than French
brandy.; whoever drinks it, is fure to be extremely agitated during the night, and to feel the next day as melancholy and reftlefs as if he had committed fome crime.

The

The true Kamtſchadales are in general below the common height; their ſhape is round and ſquat, their eyes ſmall and ſunk, their cheeks prominent, their noſe flat, their hair black, they have ſcarcely any beard, and their complexion is a little tawny. The complexion and features of the women are very nearly the ſame; from this repreſentation, it will be ſuppoſed they are not very ſeducing objeẽts.

The charaẽter of the Kamtſchadales is mild and hoſpitable; they are neither knaves, nor robbers; they have indeed ſo little penetration, that nothing is more eaſy than to deceive them, as we have ſeen in the advantage that is taken of their propenſity to intoxication. They live together in the utmoſt harmony, and the more ſo, it would ſeem, on account of the ſmallneſs of their number. This unanimity diſpoſes them to aſſiſt one another in their labours,

bours, which is no fmall proof of their zeal
to oblige, if we confider the natural and extreme flothfulnefs of their difpofition. An
active life would be infupportable to them;
and the greateft happinefs, in their eftimation, next to that of getting drunk, is to
have nothing to do, and to live for ever in
tranquil indolence. This is carried fo far
with thefe people, as frequently to make
them neglect the means of providing the
indifpenfable neceffaries of life ; and whole
families are often reduced to all the feveri-
ties of famine, becaufe they would not take
the pains of providing in fummer a referve
of fifh, without which they are unable to
live. If they neglect in this manner the
prefervation of their exiftence, it is not
to be fuppofed that they are more attentive to the article of cleanlinefs; it dif-
plays itfelf neither in their perfons, nor
their habitations ; and they may juftly be
reproached for being addicted to the contrary

trary extreme. Notwithftanding this careleffnefs, and other natural defe&ts, it muft
be regretted that their number is not more
confiderable ; as, from what I have feen,
and what has been confirmed to me by different perfons, if we would be fure of finding fentiments of honour and humanity in
this country, it is neceffary to feek for them
among the true Kamtfchadales ; they have
not yet bartered their rude virtues for the
polifhed vices of the Europeans fent to
civilize them.

It was at Bolcheretfk that I began to perceive the effe&ts of their influence. I faw
the trace of European manners, lefs in the
mixture of blood, in the conformation of
features, and the idiom of the inhabitants,
than in their inclinations and mode of life,
which did not always difcover any very
confiderable fund of virtue. This ftriking difference between the inhabitants and

the indigenes, fprings, in my opinion, from
the difficulties which lie in the road to civilization, and I will affign my reafons.

   Bolcheretfk, not long ago, was the chief
place of Kamtfchatka, particularly as the
governors had thought proper to eftablifh
their refidence there. The chiefs and their
fuites introduced European knowledge and
manners : thefe, it is known, generally become adulterated in tranfmiffion, according
to the diftance from the fource. Meanwhile it is to be prefumed that the Ruffian
government was careful, as far as it was
poffible, to confide its authority and the
execution of its orders, only to officers of
acknowledged merit, if I may judge from
thofe who are at prefent employed ; and it
is therefore to be fuppofed that thefe officers,
in the places of their refidence, were fo
many examples of the virtues, the acquire-
ments, and all the eftimable qualities of
                                                civilized

civilized nations. But unfortunately the
leffons which thy gave, were not always fo
efficacious as might have been expected;
either becaufe being only fketches, they
were not fufficiently felt, or rather, not being imbibed in all their purity, they made
but momentary or perhaps vicious impreffions on the mind.

Thefe reformers found not the fame zeal
either in the Coffacs who compofed the
garrifon, or in the merchants and other
Ruffian emigrants who fettled in the peninfula. The difpofition to licencioufnefs,
and the defire of gain, which the firft con-
querors of a country almoft always bring
with them, and the continual development
of thefe qualities, by the facility with which
the natives may be duped, contributed to
check the progefs of reform. The fatal in-
fection was ftill more diffufely fpread by
intermarriages, while the feed of the focial

H 2   virtues,

virtues, which had been attempted to be fown, fcarcely found a reception.

The confequence has been, that the natives, or true Kamtfchadales, have preferved almoft univerfally their ignorant fimplicity and uncultivated manners; and that a part of the reft of the inhabitants, Ruffians and mixed breed, who have fettled themfelves in the oftrogs where the governors refide, ftill retain indeed a faint fhade of European manners, but not of fuch as are moft pure. We have already had a proof of this in what has been faid of their commercial principles, and my conviction has been rendered ftronger during my abode at Bolcheretfk, by a clofer ftudy of the inhabitants, who, this faint fhade excepted, differ little from the indigenes.

M. Kafloff, and thofe who accompanied him, in imitation of his example, frequently

give

give entertainments or balls to the ladies of
this oftrog, who accept fuch invitations with
equal alacrity and joy. I had an opportunity of feeing that what I had been told
was true; that thefe women, the Kamtfchadales as well as the Ruffians, have a ftrong
propenfity to pleafure; their eagernefs indeed is fo great, that they are unable to
conceal it. The precofity of the girls is
aftonifhing, and feems not at all to be affected by the coldnefs of the climate.

With refpect to the women of Bolcheretfk, who were prefent at thefe affemblies,
and who were chiefly either of mixed blood
or of Ruffian parents, their figures in general did not appear difagreeable, and I perceived fome who might be confidered as
handfome: but the frefhnefs of youth is
not of long duration; from child-bearing,
or the painful labours to which they are
fubjected, it fades away almoft in the flower

H 3   of

of their age. Their difpofition is extremely
cheerful ; a little, perhaps, at the expence
of decency. They endeavour to amufe the
company by every thing which their gaiety
and playfulnefs can furnifh. They are fond
of finging, and their voice is pleafant and
agreeable ; it is only to be wifhed that their
mufic had lefs refemblance to their foil, and
approached nearer to our own. They fpeak
both the Ruffian and Kamtfchadale languages, but they all preferve the accent of
the latter idiom. I little expected to fee
in this part of the world Polifh dances, and
ftill lefs country dances in the Englifh
tafte ; but what was my furprife to find
that they had even an idea of a minuet !
Whether my abode for twenty fix months
upon the fea, had rendered me lefs faftidi-
ous, or that the recollections they revived
facinated my eyes, thefe dances appeared to
be executed with tolerable precifion, and
more grace than I could have imagined.

The

The dancers of whom we fpeak, have fo much vanity as to hold in contempt the fongs and dances of the natives. The toilet of the women on thefe occafions is an object of no trivial attention. They deck themfelves out in all their allurements, and whatever is moft coftly. Thefe ceremonious and ball dreffes are principally of filks; and in the article of commerce we have already feen that they muft be expenfive. I fhall finifh this account with a remark that I had occafion to make, both in thefe affemblies and in thofe of the Kamtfchadales; it is, that the majority of hufbands, Ruffians as well as natives, are not fufceptible of jealoufy; they voluntarily fhut their eyes upon the conduct of their wives, and are as docile as poffible upon this chapter.

The entertainments and affemblies of the native Kamtfchadales, at which I was alfo

prefent,

prefent, offered a fpectacle equally entitled to notice for its fingularity. I know
not which ftruck me moft, the fong or the
dance. The dance appeared to me to be
that of favages. It confifted in making regular movements, or rather unpleafant and
difficult diftortions, and in uttering at the
fame time a forced and gutteral found,
like a continued hiccough, to mark the
time of the air fung by the affembly, the
words of which are frequently void of fenfe,
even in Kamtfchadale. I noted down one
of thefe airs, which I fhall infert in this
place, in order to give an idea of their
mufic and metre.

Daria, Daria, da, Daria, ha, nou
dalatché, damatché, kannha, koukka.

Da Capo.

The

The words mean,

Daria *, Daria fings and dances ftill.

This air is repeated without ceafing.

In their dances they are fond of imitat-
ing the different animals they purfue, fuch
as the partridge and others, but principally
the bear. They reprefent its fluggifh and
ftupid gait, its different feelings and fitua-
tions; as the young ones about their dam;
the amourous fports of the male with the
female; and laftly, its agitation when purfued. They muft have a perfect knowledge
of this animal, and have made it their particular ftudy, for they reprefent all its motions as exactly, I believe, as it is poffible.
I afked the Ruffians, who were greater
connoiffeurs than myfelf, having been oftener prefent at the taking of thefe animals,

* Daria is a female Ruffian name.

whether

whether their pantomime ballets were well executed ; and they affured me that the dancers were the beft in the country, and that the cries, gait, and various attitudes of the bear, were as accurate as life. Meanwhile, without offence to the amateurs, thefe dances are, in my opinion, not lefs fatiguing to the fpectators than to the performers. It is a real pain to fee them diftort their hips, diflocate every limb, and wear out their lungs, to exprefs the excefs of pleafure which they take in thefe ftrange balls, which, I repeat it, refemble the abfurd diverfions of favages : the Kamtfchadales may indeed, in many refpects, be confidered as of that rank.

Having given an account of the addrefs with which thefe people counterfeit the poftures and motions of the bear, who may be called their dancing mafter, it may not be unpleafing to relate in what manner they hunt

IN KAMTSCHATKA. 107

hunt this animal. There are various modes
of attacking it; fometimes they lay fnares
for it: under a heavy trap, fupported in
the air by a fcaffolding fufficiently high,
they place fome kind of bait to attract the
bear, and which he no fooner fmells and
perceives, than he eagerly advances to devour; at the fame time he fhakes the feeble
fupport of the trap, which falls upon his
neck, and punifhes his voracioufnefs by
crufhing his head, and frequently his whole
body. In paffing the woods I have feen
them caught in this way; the trap is
kept baited till it fucceeds, which fometimes does not happen for almoft a year.
This method of taking them requires no
great boldnefs, or fatigue; but there is
another mode, very much adopted in this
country, to which equal ftrength and courage are neceffary. A Kamtfchadale goes
out, either alone or in company, to find a
bear. He has no other arms than his gun,
a kind

a kind of carabine whofe but-end is very fmall; a lance or fpear; and his knife. His ftock of provifion is made up in a bundle containing about twenty fifh. Thus lightly equipped, he penetrates into the thickeft part of the woods, and every place that is likely to be the haunt of this annimal. It is commonly in the briars, or among the rufhes on the borders of lakes and rivers, that the Kamtfchadale pofts himfelf, and waits the approach of his adverfary with patience and intrepidity; if it be neceffary, he will remain thus in ambufcade for a whole week together, till the bear makes his appearance. The moment it comes within his reach, he fixes in the ground a forked ftick* belonging to his gun, by means of which he takes a truer aim, and fhoots with

---

* The Kamtfchadales are unable to fhoot without this means of refting their gun, which, from the time required to prepare it, is evidently inconfiftent with the celerity of this inftrument, its chief advantage to a fportfman.

more

more certainty. It is feldom that, with
the fmalleft ball, he does not ftrike the bear
either in the head, or near the fhoulder,
which is the tendereft part. But he is obliged to charge again inftantly, becaufe the
bear, if the firft fhot has not difabled him,
runs* at the hunter, who has not always
time for a fecond fhot. He has then recourfe to his lance, with which he quickly
arms himfelf to contend with the beaft, who
attacks him in his turn. His life is in danger † if he does not give the bear a mortal
thruft; and in fuch combats, it may be fup-

* It is common enough alfo for it to take to flight, notwithftanding its wound, and conceal itfelf in thickets or
rufhes, where it is traced by means of its blood, and found
either dead or expiring,

† I was affured that when a bear triumphs over his ag-
greffor, he tears the fkin from the fkull, draws it over his
face, and then leaves him ; a mode of revenge which implies, according to the Kamtfchadales, that this animal cannot bear the human afpect ; and this ftrange prejudice fupports them in the opinion of their fuperiority, and feems to
infpire them with additional courage.

pofed

pofed the man is not always the conqueror;
but this does not prevent the inhabitants
of this country from daily expofing their
lives; the frequent examples of the death
of their countrymen has no effect upon
them: indeed they never go out, without
confidering before hand that it is either to
conquer or to die; and this fevere alterna-
tiue neither ftops nor terrifies them*.

They hunt other animals nearly in the
fame manner, fuch as rein deer, argali, or
wild fheep, called in Ruffia *diki-barani*,

---

* They hunt the bear in this manner in every feafon of
the year, except when the country is covered with fnow;
their method is then different. It is known that in winter
the bear retreats to the den which he has fabricated during
fummer of the branches of trees; he continues there while
the froft lafts, either afleep, or licking his paws. The
Kamtfchadales purfue him in their fledges, and attack him
with their dogs, who oblige him to defend himfelf: he
rufhes from his lurking place to certain death; if he refufe to come out, his fate is equally certain, and he is
crufhed to death under the ruins of his den.

foxes,

foxes, otters, beavers, fables, hares*, &c.
but they have not the fame dangers to encounter ; fometimes they make ufe of fnares,
conftructed of wood or iron, lefs than thofe
which are fet for bears, and refembling in
their fimplicity our pitfalls ; no other attention is neceffary than that of vifiting
them from time to time. The Kamtfchadales fometimes lie in ambufh, armed in the
manner I have defcribed ; and the only
hardfhip they experience refults from their
provifion being exhaufted in confequence
of the long duration of their chace. They
frequently fubmit to fuffer hunger for many
days together, rather than quit their fta-
tions till they have obtained the end of their
purfuit ; but they amply repay themfelves
for this fafting, by immediately devouring
the flefh of the animals †, and by the plea-

* Thefe animals are all defcribed in Cook's voyage.

† The flefh of bears, argali, and rain-deer, is confidered
by them as very wholefome, the laft particularly ; I frequently feafted upon it.

fure

fure with which they count over the fkins
they obtain from them.

They chufe for their chace the feafons
when the fur of the animal is in its greateft
perfection. Sables are hunted in the be-
ginning of winter. Thefe animals live
commonly in trees, and are called after
their name ; a part of the fur neareft the
fkin being of the fame colour as thofe which
they moft frequent, as the birch, the fir, &c.

The moft. favourable feafons for hunting
foxes are autumn, winter, and fpring. There
are four different fpecies. 1. The whitifh
red fox, which is leaft efteemed. 2. The
red or bright red fox. 3. The fox called
févadoufchka, the colour of which is a mixture of red, black, and grey. 4. The black
fox, which is the fcarceft and moft valuable:
it is really of a deep and entire black, except that at the extremity of the fur upon
the

the back, which is the longeſt; a grey tint
is ſometimes perceptible. Some of this ſpecies are ſingularly valuable. There are
two other ſpecies of the fox that may be
added to theſe, though they are not regarded as ſuch in this country, the blue fox
and the white fox. They are called in
Ruſſia *galouboy peſſets*, and *beloy peſſets*; their
fur is thicker than that of the reſt of the
ſpecies. The foxes of the continent are in
general more beautiful than thoſe caught in
the different iſlands of the eaſt*, and produce an infinitely higher price.

Rein-deer are hunted in winter, and argali in autumn. Otters are extremely
ſcarce in this country; but there is a great
abundance of ermines, though, I know not
for what reaſon, no pains are taken to catch

* The Aleutienne iſlands, Schoumagine iſlands, Fox
iſlands, &c.

them ; one would fuppofe they were of no
value.

The Kamtfchadales have different feafons
alfo for fifhing. Their falmon and trout
feafon is in June, their herring feafon in
May, and that of the fea wolf in fpring
and fummer, but principally in autumn.

They feldom ufe feines, but almoft always
common nets *, or a kind of harpoon, which
they manage with great dexterity. Seines
ferve only for fea wolves; they are made
of leather ftraps, and the mefhes are very
large. They have another mode of fifhing,

---

* Their nets are made-of pack thread, like ours ; they
purchafe it of the Ruffians : there is another kind however,
which they fabricate themfelves from nettles, of which they
take care to lay up a confiderable ftore. They gather them
in autumn, tie them in bundles, and place them under their
balagans to dry. When their fifhing and harvefts are compleated, they prepare their nettles. They flit them, and
then ftrip off the rind expertly with their teeth ; the reft
they beat and fhake till the filaments are feparated, and it
is fit for fpinning.

by

by clofing up the river with ftakes and
branches of trees, fo as to leave only a narrow paffage for the fifh, or fometimes feveral,
where they place bafkets, fo conftructed that,
if the fifh once enter, it is impoffible for
them to retreat.

Horfes are very fcarce in Kamtfchatka.
I faw fome at Bolcheretfk belonging to government, and intrufted to the care of the
Coffacs. They merely ferve during fummer for the carriage of merchandize and
other effects of the crown, and for the convenience of travellers.

Dogs however abound in this country,
and are fo ferviceable to the Kamtfchadales,
as to render the privation of the other do-
meftic animals lefs felt by them. They ferve
all the purpofes of carriage, and are fed without difficulty or expence, their food confifting entirely of the offals, or fuch decayed

I 2   fifh

fifh as are rejected by their mafters; and
even thefe are not allowed, unlefs when it
is neceffary. In fummer, which is their
feafon of reft, little care is taken of them;
the dogs well know how to provide for
themfelves, by ranging over the country
and along the fides of lakes and rivers; and
the punctuality with which they return, is
one of the moft ftriking proofs of the fide-
lity of thefe animals. When winter arrives,
they dearly pay for the liberty and tempo-
rary repofe they have enjoyed. Their labour and flavery begin anew, and thefe dogs
muft have extreme vigour to be able to fupport them. Ma nwhile they are not re-
markably large, and refemble pretty exactly our mountain dogs, or fuch as are
commonly ufed by fhepherds. There is
not an individual inhabitant, Ruffian or
native, that has lefs than five. They make
ufe of them when they travel, when they go
to the forefts to cut wood, and for the conveyance

veyance of their effects and provifions, as
well as their perfons. In fhort, thefe dogs
conduct travellers from place to place, and
horfes could not in reality be more ferviceable. They are harneffed to a fledge
two and two together*, with a fingle one
before as a leader. This honour is beftowed
on the moft intelligent, or the beft trained
dog, and he underftands wonderfully the
terms ufed by the conductor to direct his
courfe. The cry of *tagtag, tagtag*, turns
him to the right, and *kougha, kougha*, to the
left; the intelligent animal underftands it

---

* They are caftrated like horfes, but the mode of per-
forming the operation is different. The Kamtfchadales do
not extirpate the tefticles, but bruife them, and the inftrument they make ufe of is their teeth. Some of them do
not furvive, and others are crippled and unfit for fervice.
In the mean time it is imagined that equal advantage could
not be derived from thefe animals, if they were permitted
to remain in their natural ftate; it would not be practica-
ble to harnefs them with females. All the males, however,
are not mutilated; a fufficient number is referved for the
prefervation of the fpecies, and thefe are frequently ufed for
hunting.

imme-

immediately, and gives to the reft the example of obedience: *ah, ah,* ftops them, and
ha makes them fet off. The number of
dogs that it is neceffary to harnefs, depends
upon the load ; when it is little more than
the weight of the perfon who mounts the
fledge, it is confidered as a common fledge, or
faunka*, and the team confifts of four or five
dogs. The harnefs† is made of leather.
It paffes under the neck, that is, upon the
breaft of thefe fteeds, and is joined to the
fledge by a ftrap three feet long, in the
manner of a trace : the dogs are alfo faftened together by couples paffed through their
collars ; thefe collars are frequently covered
with bear's fkin, by way of ornament.

The form of the fledge is like that of an

* The fledges for baggage are called *narta,* and are drawn
by ten dogs.

† Called *alaki.*

oblong

oblong baſket, the two extremities of which
are elevated in a curve.   Its length is about
three feet, and its breadth ſcarcely exceeds
a foot.   This kind of baſket, which com-
poſes the body of the ſledge, is of very thin
wood ; the ſides are of open work, and ornamented with ſtraps of different colours.
The ſeat of the charioteer is covered with
bear's ſkin, and elevated three feet from the
ground, upon four legs, which diverge towards the lower extremity, and are faſtened
to two parallel planks, three or four inches
broad.   Theſe planks are not thick, but ſo
long as to extend beyond the body of the
ſledge, to which they ſerve as ſupports and
and as ſkates. For this purpoſe they are furniſhed underneath, in time of thaw, with
three or four long pieces of whale-bone, all
of them of the ſame breadth, and faſtened to
the ſkates with leathern thongs. In front
theſe planks bend upward, and ſo meet the
poles of the ſledge, which gradually lo ver

for that purpofe, and are adapted to receive
a part of the baggage. The front of the
fledge is farther adorned with floating reins
or fhreds of leather, which are of no ufe.
The charioteer has nothing in his hand but
a curved ftick, which ferves him both for
rudder and whip. Iron rings are fufpended
at one end of the ftick, as much for ornament, as to encourage the dogs by the noife
which thefe kind of bells make, and which
are frequently jingled for that purpofe;
the other end is fometimes pointed with iron,
to make an eafier impreffion on the ice, and
ferves at the fame time to guide the ardour
of thefe animals. Dogs, that are well trained, have no need to hear the voice of the
conductor; if he ftrike the ice with his
ftick, they will go to the left; if he ftrike
the legs of the fledge, they will go to the
right; and when he wifhes them to flop,
he has only to place the ftick between the
fnow and the front of the fledge. When
they

they flacken their pace, and become carelefs
and inattentive to the fignals, or to his voice,
he throws his ftick at them*; but then the
utmoft addrefs is neceffary to regain it, as
he proceeds rapidly along; and this is one
of the ftrongeft tefts of the fkill of the conductor. The Kamtfchadales are fingularly
expert in this exercife. I was in general
aftonifhed at the dexterity they difplayed in
driving their fledges, and as I was foon to
have the happinefs of travelling in this vehicle, I conceived that I ought to practice,
not fo much to reconcile myfelf to it, as to
learn to be my own guide. It was in vain
they reprefented to me the rifks I fhould
run, by expofing myfelf alone in a fledge,
before I had acquired fufficient fkill to know
how to conduct it; at my age we are all
confident, and I liftened not to their cau-
tions. The lightnefs of my carriage, which
fcarcely exceeded ten pounds, its elevation,

* This ftick is called *ofchtol*.

which

which rendered it more liable to be overturned, the difficulty of preferving the
equilibrium, and, in fhort, the confequences
that might attend a fall, if I loft my hold of
the fledge*; all thefe confiderations, which
were expofed to my view, could neither in-
timidate nor diffuade me from fo dangerous
an apprenticefhip.   I mounted one day my
new car, confenting however to be followed, and a multitude of fledges attended me.
It was not long before the company faw
their predictions realized; I had advanced
a very little way, when I exhibited a complete fall.   Scarcely remounted, I repeated
the fcene, and occafioned a new burft of
laughter : in fpite of this, I did not lofe my
courage, but quickly recovered myfelf to be
overturned again as quickly.   I had fufficient reafon to be inured to thefe acci-

* The dogs feeling their burthen become lighter, advance with fuch fpeed as frequently not to ftop till they have
exhaufted themfelves with fatigue, or dafhed the fledge to
pieces againft the trees.

dents,

dents, for in every attempt I paid the tribute of inexperience. Seven times did I fall
in taking my firſt leſſon, but without receiving any injury ; and I only returned
with more eagernefs to take a ſecond, then a
third, then a fourth ; in ſhort, a day ſcarcely paſſed, without my making ſome progrefs. The number of my falls diminiſhed,
in proportion as I acquired more knowledge
and ſkill, and my ſuccefs rendered me ſuch
an amateur of this exercife, that in a ſhort
time I acquired a degree of reputation ; it
coſt me, however, conſiderable pains to ha-
bituate myſelf to the obſervance of the neceſſary equilibrium. The body is, as it
were, in continual motion. Here we muſt
lean to the right, becaufe the ſledge inclines
to the left ; there we muſt ſuddenly change
to the left, becaufe it leans to the right :
the next minute, perhaps our poſture muſt
be erect ; and if we fail in quicknefs or attention, it is ſeldom that an immediate overthrow

throw is not the confequence. In falling, it is ftill neceffary not to quit the vehicle, but to hold it as firm as poffible, in order to create a fufficient weight to impede the dogs, who, as I have already faid, will other- wife advance full fpeed. The common mode of fitting in a fledge is fide ways, as a lady rides on horfeback; we may alfo fit aftride; but the point of main difficulty, the *ne plus ultra* of addrefs and of grace, is to be able to ftand upon one leg: it is excellent to fee an adept in this ftriking attitude.

For myfelf, I was no fooner able to drive, than I abandoned every other mode of con- veyance. Always accompanied, becaufe of the roads, I fometimes took a ride, and fometimes went a hunting. The tracks of hares and partridges were perceptible on the fnow*, and to fuch a degree, that it ap- peared

* The fnow began to fall 5 November, and fo heavily, that the country was covered almoft immediately. But the froft

peared full of holes like a fieve. The fnow was frequently fo deep in the woods, that it was impoffible to proceed a ftep without finking in; our refource in that cafe was to quit our fledges, which were no longer ferviceable to us, and turn them upon their fide. Having taking this precaution, which was fufficient to retain our dogs, who immediately laid themfelves down in a circular form upon the fnow, and patiently waited the return of their guides; we faftened to the foles of our feet, with leathern thongs, rackets, made of thin board *, fix or eight inches wide and four feet long, the front of which turned up like fkates, and the bot-

froft being later, and gufts of wind continuing almoft without ceffation, the fledges could not conveniently be ufed till a confiderable time after, as will be feen in the fequel.

* Thefe rackets are called *ligi*. In the northern part of the peninfula they ufe another fort of racket, called *lapki*, which are fhorter, and made of leathern thorns twifted, like the ftrings of a tennis racket; two fmall fharp pointed bones are fixed in the bottom, which penetrate the ice, and are a prefervative againft fliding.

tom

tom was covered with the fkin of the fea wolf or rein deer. Furnifhed with thefe kind of fhoes, we continued our chace; I had at firft fome difficulty to accuftom myfelf to them, and I fell more than once both upon my back and my face; but the pleafure of a good chace made me foon forget thefe accidents. Though it was difficult to perceive the hares and partridges, whofe whitenefs equalled that of the fnow, I did not fail, after a little practice, and fome inftructions from my companions, to bring home a tolerable number.

This was one of my moft agreeable diverfions while at Bolcheretfk; the reft of my hours were occupied in expreffing my impatience and uneafinefs, on account of the length of time I was obliged to ftay there. To give a different turn to my thoughts, I embraced the few fine days that we experienced, to vifit fome of the environs,

which

which I had a fecond opportunity of viewing upon my departure, and which I fhall
mention when I proceed on my travels.
The conftruction of my travelling fledges*
engaged alfo my attention; but my chief confolation was the company of M. Kafloff and
the officers of his fuite. Their converfations, and the enquiries which I made, enabled me almoft every day to take notes, a
part of which I have already tranfcribed,
and fhall now proceed with the reft.

The difeafes that prevail in Kamtfchatka
is the firft article that prefents itfelf. Difagreeable as may be the details they require, I conceive that I ought not to fupprefs them; they form a part of my obfervations, and fhould have a place in my
journals.

* A kind of clofe coach to fleep in, and which is fitted
to the fledge. It is like a carriage very common in Ruffia,
called *vezok*; mine was lined with bear's fkin, and covered
with the fkin of the fea wolf.

The

The fmall pox, whofe ravages I have already mentioned, appears not to be natural
to the country, nor is it very common.
Since the invafion of the Ruffians, and the
frequent emigrations that fucceeded it, this
epidemical difeafe has only made its appearance in 1767 and 1768. It was then
brought into the country by a Ruffian veffel bound to the Eaftern iflands, for the
purpofe of hunting otters, foxes, and other
animals. The perfon, who had in his blood
the fatal germ, was a failor from Okotfk,
where he had taken remedies for the diforder, previous to his departure; but the
recent marks of it were vifible. Scarcely
landed, he communicated this cruel malady
to the poor Kamtfchadales, which carried
off three fourths of them. As it has not appeared fince, it is fuppofed that thefe people
are not fubject to it. In the year 1720 it
broke out in the northern part of Kamtfchatka, but it did not fpread fo far as the
peninfula.

peninfula. It began at Anadirfkoi ; it is
not known how it was brought there,
though the Ruffians are alfo accufed in this
inftance.

There is reafon to fufpect that the Kamtfchadales are indebted to them in like man-
nner for their knowledge of the venereal
difeafe, which happily is not common.
This peftilence appears to be exotic, and its
cure is as difficult as it is rare. They have
recourfe to various roots and to corrofive
fublimate, which is attended in this country with its ufual ruinous effects, and the
more fo, as being indifcreetly adminiftered.

The Kamtfchadales have no deformed
births. Such as are deformed among them,
have become fo in confequence of a confiderable fall, though this is not a very common occurrence, as they are accuftomed to
fall from their balagans. They are but

little fubject to the fcurvy; their ufe of
wild garlic, and various fruits and berries, is
a prefervative. The Ruffians and other
fettlers are more frequently afflicted with
this difeafe.

Confumptions are frequent enough; but
boils, tumors, abfceffes, and wens, are very
common. They have no mode of curing
them, but by incifion or extirpation; and
they ufe for thefe operations a knife, or
perhaps fimply a fharp ftone, which fupplies the place of a lancet. Such inftruments are calculated to imprefs us with no
very high opinion of the fkill of the ope-
rators; and it is obvious that the art of
furgery, brought to fuch perfection with
us, is in a ftate of the utmoft barbarifm at
Kamtfchatka.

Phyfic does not appear to have made a
greater progrefs; though it muft be con-
feffed

feffed that thefe people have gained fomething by learning to diftruft their impoftors
and abfurd empiricks. Formerly, felf-created magicians, called *chamans*, taking advantage of the credulity of the Kamtfchadales, turned doctors of phyfic, and thus
fecured to themfelves a double claim to
their veneration and confidence *. Their
ftrange drefs contributed to the impofition,
and fuited perfectly their extravagant mum-
meries. What was told me upon the fubject would exceed the utmoft ftretch of
faith, if we had never heard of the Bohe-
mians and other forcerers of this kind. It
is not poffible to form an idea of the buffooneries of thefe fuppofitious phyficians,
and the impertinencies they relate, to make
their prefcriptions or pretended revelations
go down. It is probable that their cures

* In an oftrog at fome diftance from Bolcheretfk, I had
afterwards an opportunity of confidering this fubject more
fully, and my obfervations will be found in their proper
place.

were frequently attended with fatal confequences, and that the number of victims
equalled that of their patients. Tired at
laſt of being duped at the expence of their
lives, the Kamtſchadales began to be dif-
ſatisfied with theſe impoſtors, who gradually loſt their credit, and ſunk into contempt and oblivion. Such has been the
fate alſo of the chamans. The feeble light
which the Ruſſian commerce diffuſed through
the country, proved ſufficient to open the
eyes of the inhabitants. They perceived
at once the abſurdity of the magic art of
their doctors. As it ceaſed to be reſpected, it
was no longer lucrative, and the number
of magicians diminiſhed of courſe. Dif-
guſted with the trade, the men abandoned
it ; and it has ſince been taken up by ſome
old women, who, poſſeſſing leſs ſkill, have
doubtleſs fewer cuſtomers *.

The

* The revolution which took place in Kamtſchatka
reſpecting the chamans, is the preciſe hiſtory of all our
mountebanks.

The women of this country have feldom
more than ten children, the common eftimate is four or five, they bear none after the age of forty. They affift one another in their deliveries, which are effected
with great facility : meanwhile there are
midwives in Kamtfchatka, but their number is very fmall. The accidents which
prove fatal to fo many mothers; are much
lefs frequent to thefe women, than inftances
of child-birth in the open air, in roads, or
wherever their occupations call them. On

mountebanks. Similar in their impoftures, their reign
and their fall are fimilar. Various reflections might be
made on this fubject. That a people equally fimple and
uninformed, like the Kamtfchadales, fhould for a time
have been the dupes of the impoftures of their magicians,
is not aftonifhing, and will admit of an excufe : but that
fuch extreme ignorance and credulity fhould be made fenfible of their error, and blufh at it, is a matter of furprife
and congratulation ; for even with the moft enlightened
nations of Europe, do not fome kinds of chamans fpring up
every day, equally perfidious and deftructive! They have
all in the mean time their apoftles, their profelytes, and a
prodigious number of martyrs,

K 3   thefe

thefe occafions they make ufe of their hair,
I am told, to tie the umbilical cord, carry
home their children themfelves, and immediately give them fuck. They have no
limited time for fuckling their children,
and I have feen inftances of its continuing
for four or five years. We may judge from
this circumftance of the ftrong conftitution
of thefe women. It is obferved, however,
that Kamtfchadales of either fex, do not
live longer than Ruffians.

I forgot to mention a remedy to which
the inhabitants of this peninfula have vo-
luntary recourfe in almoft every difeafe :
it is to a root called *bears root*, which they
fteep in brandy. The name fufficiently in-
dicates to whom they are indebted for its
knowledge. Perceiving that the bear was
fond of eating this herb, and of rolling
himfelf upon it when wounded, they imagined it to poffefs fome healing quality, and
this

this induced them to make ufe of it. This
animal thus gave them their firft leffon in
botany and pharmacy. It is faid however,
that the bear cures all his wounds with
this root. If this be true, it is natural to
fuppofe that human beings would find it
very ferviceable: but as I have never had
occafion to make the experiment, I can only
fpeak from report.

The Chriftian religion was introduced
into this country by the Ruffians ; but the
inhabitants appear to know little more of
it than the ceremony of baptifm. They
are ignorant of the very firft principles of
Chriftianity. Slaves to their inclinations,
they follow their impulfe whether good or
bad. If they think of religion, it is merely
from a motive of convenience or intereft, or
when particular circumftances compel them
to it. This proves how very defective their
inftruction is, and reflects in my opinion

K 4 upon

upon the clergy, whofe bufinefs it is to en-
lighten their ignorance. But are thefe cle-
rical miffionaries fufficiently informed themfelves? They have no opportunity it muft
be acknowledged for profound ftudy, and
probably it is not required of them, as it is
common enough to fee a Kamtfchadale ad-
mitted to this dignified office.

Thefe popes are all under the authority
of a protapope, or high prieft, refident at
Nijenei, and he again is fubordinate to the
archbifhop of Irkoutfk, who alone ordains
and appoints the clergy to their cures, fo
that they are all obliged to refort to this
fettlement. The length and perils of the
journey are confidered perhaps as a kind of
initiation; and without any other merit or
examination, they probably receive holy
orders: it is certain they return neither
wifer nor better. Thefe divines are then
fent to their places of deftination; the

time

time they continue is not limited, and depends on the will of their chiefs.

There are eight principal churches in
Kamtſchatka : Paratounka, Bolcheretſk,
Jchinſk, ı̇ iguil, Vercknei, Klutchefskaïa,
and two at Nijenei ; to theſe may be added
the church of Ingiga, in the country of the
Koriacs.

The diſtrict or pariſh of Paratounka in-
cludes ſeven oſtrogs and the Kurilles iſlands;
viz. the oſtrog of the ſame name, Saint
Peter and Saint Paul, Koriaki, Natchikin,
Apatchin, Malkin, and Bolcheretſk. The
number of pariſhioners contained in theſe
oſtrogs, does not exceed four hundred ;
and including the Kurilles iſlands, the general calculation is not more than ſix hundred and twenty Chriſtians. The rector
of Paratounka is allowed by the empreſs a

falary

falary of eighty roubles, and twenty *pouds* *
of rye flour. His parifhioners of confequence, pay no tythes ; but he receives
alms and other cafual emoluments attached
to his church. For a marriage, a chriften-
ing, or a burial, thefe priefts demand whatever they pleafe. There is no regulation
in this refpect, and every thing is governed
folely by their caprice, which occafions confiderable impofitions and abufes. In general however, they endeavour to proportion
their demands to the abilities of their parifhioners, a difcretion that is entitled to
applaufe.

The Kamtfchadales are free. They are
fubject only to an annual tribute to Ruffia,
which confifts, as I have already faid, in
various kinds of furs ; fo that the produce
of their chace, turns almoft entirely to the

* A Ruffian weight equal to about thirty-three pounds.

advantage

advantage of the emprefs. Every chief of
a family is obliged to furnifh for himfelf
and for each of his children, even fuch as
are in their minority, a certain quantity
of fkins equivalent to his fhare of taxa-
tion : this may amount to feven roubles
more or lefs, and the fkins, I am told, are
generally valued at the loweft poffible price.
This mode of paying tribute muft produce
a confiderable revenue to the crown, if we
merely judge from the number of fables the
province annually fupplies, which is fomething more than four thoufand. The toyon
of each oftrog collects the taxes, and re-
mits them to the treafurer of the crown ; a
receipt is previoufly given to every individual of the amount of his tribute, and each
Kamtfchadale takes care to mark with his
feal, or fome other fign, all the furs that he
delivers.

The current coins are the golden imperial
of

of ten roubles ; the rouble, and half rouble.
There are very few filver coins below this
value ; a proof that no article of merchandize is expected to produce lefs than half
a rouble. Copper and paper money have
not yet reached this peninfula. A variety
of old filver coins of the times of Peter I.
Catherine I. and Elizabeth, abound here.
A confiderable branch of commerce may be
made of them ; the filver is purer and more
valuable than that of common coins.

The pay of the foldiers or Coffacs is
fifteen roubles a year. The officers fent by
government to fo diftant a country, receive
double falaries.

The peninfula of Kamtfchatka, when
major Behm prefided at Bolcheretfk, was
under the jurifdiction of the government
general of Irkoutfk. Upon the departure
of this governor, whom the Englifh faw
upon

upon their firft arrival in 1779, captain
Schmaleff was deputed in his room, and
enjoyed for a year the power and fatisfaction of doing good to the inhabitants, who
entertain for him an equal refpect and gratitude. M. Renikin fupplied his place in
1780, and was recalled in 1784 for reafons
which I am obliged to fupprefs. At this
period the Kamtfchatka department was
reunited to that of Okotfk. The chiefs
and officers of the different oftrogs have
fince been fubject to the orders of the governor at Okotfk, and to the decifions of
its courts of juftice; thefe are themfelves
fubordinate and accountable to the governor general refiding at Irkoutfk. The prefent commanding officer, or governor, at Bolcheretfk, which was formerly the capital of
Kamtfchatka, is now merely a fergeant; the
name of the perfon I left there was *Raftar-
gouieff*, and he had been nominated to the
office by M. Kafloff.

The

The governors in thefe various oftrogs are not accountable to one another for their adminiftration, not even inferior officers to their fuperiors; the authority of each is limited to the inhabitants of his own diftrict; which has doubtlefs induced the emprefs to appoint an infpector general, *capitan ifpravnick*, whofe bufinefs is to vfiit every year all the Kamtfchadale villages, receive their complaints, examine their differences, judge them, and punifh fuch as are guilty; in fhort to maintain order and peace among them. It is alfo a duty of his function to encourage commerce, particularly their fifhing and hunting, to infpect the regular payment of their tribute, the ftock of provifions of each individual for his own fupport, and that of his family, the repairs of the bridges and roads, which unfortunately are very few, and kept in very bad order. In a word, the infpector general fhould confider it as incumbent upon him to introduce

among

among thefe people the manners and cuftoms of Ruffia. This important office was
confided, in 1784, to baron de Steinheil,
who fixed his refidence at Nijenei. Affairs
calling him elfewhere, he was fucceeded by
M. Schmaleff, who, in accompanying us,
was making the tour of his office.

The government is not purely military;
there are fome tribunals eftablifhed for hearing and deciding caufes and other matters
juridically. Such are the tribunals of Tiguil,
Ingiga, and Nijenei-Kamtfchatka; they are
fubject to the jurifdiction of the court of
Okotfk, in the fame manner as in Ruffia
the magiftrates of the fubordinate towns
hold from thofe of the capital, in whom
the final decifion refts. There is befide at
Bolcheretfk a kind of confular jurifdiction,
or vocal tribunal, called in Ruffia *Slovefnoi-
foud*. The judges are merchants; they take
cognizance of all difputes relating to commerce,

merce, and their decifions are either confirmed or annulled by the court to which
they are carried by appeal. The Ruffian
code of laws is the only one that is attended to; it is too well known to require that
I fhould enter into particulars; and I could
only repeat what has been already related
by various hiftorians and travellers better
informëd upon the fubject than myfelf.

I ought however to add, that the property of the Kamtfchadales devolves, of
courfe, upon their deceafe, to the next heir,
or to whomfoever it is bequeathed. The
will of the teftator is equally refpected, and
as literally adhered to, as it could be with
thofe nations of Europe who are moft fcrupulous on the fubject of fucceffions.

Divorces are neither practifed or allowed
among the Kamtfchadales. The Ruffians
feem to court their alliance, though it pro-
cures

cures them no particular priviledge. Their motive is obvious. By frequent marriages, it is poffible that before the end of the pre-fent generation, the race of the indigenes may be totally extinct

The penalty of death, abolifhed in all the dominions of the emprefs, is never inflicted in Kamtfchatka. In their earlieft migrati-ons, the Ruffians, when accufed of haraffing the natives, were condemned to the knowt; the Kamtfchadales alfo, for various offences, were liable to this cruel punifhment; but it is no longer practiced. When the natives are guilty either of petty or capital offences, the punifhment is whipping. It may be queftioned whether they have gained by the change. The prefent mode of punifhing them being more fimple and expeditious, it is reforted to with lefs fcruple, and is liable to frequent abufe.

The Kamtfchadale idiom appeared to me
to be uncouth, guttural, and difficult to be
pronounced; the words are broken, and the
founds difagreeable. There are as many
different dialects and accents as there are
oftrogs. For inftance, upon leaving Saint
Peter and Saint Paul, we are aftonifhed to
hear a different jargon at Paratounka: this
is the cafe with villages the neareft to one
another. Notwithftanding thefe variations
of idiom, I confidered it as incumbent upon
me to procure a vocabulary, which will be
found at the end of my journal. I fhall
add to it the Koriac, the Tchouktchi, and
the Lamout languages. My attention to the
fubject was unremitted, and I received very
confiderable affiftance. I fhall finifh the article of my abode at Bolcheretfk, with fome
obfervations that will tend to prove the
impoffibility of my leaving it fooner.

Towards the end of November the cold
became

became on a fudden fo fevere, that in a few
days the rivers were all frozen, even the Bolchaïa-reka, which feldom happens, becaufe
of the extreme rapidity of its current. The
next day it got rid of the ice that covered
it, and from that time I faw no more ftop
before Bolcheretfk, lower than the houfe of
the governor. Though frozen in various
places, it prefents a great number chafms,
where the water is feen to flow as ufual.

On each fhore of the peninfula, there
is a fenfible difference in the atmofphere.
During the fine weather, a drought prevailed at Saint Peter and Saint Paul's, whereas at Bolcheretfk they complained of frequent fhowers ; meanwhile autumn had not
proved this year more rainy than common. Very heavy rains are injurious in
this country, becaufe they occafion floods,
which drive the fifh from the rivers; a famine moft diftreffing to the poor Kamt-

L 2   fchadales

fchadales is the refult, as it happened laft
year in all the villages along the weftern
coaft of the peninfula. This dreadful calamity occurs fo frequently in this quarter,
that the inhabitants are obliged to abandon their dwellings, and repair with their
families to the borders of the Kamtfchatka,
where they hope to find better refources,
fifh being more plentiful in this river. M.
Kafloff had intended to proceed along the
weftern coaft, having already made his vifit
through the eaft; but the news of this famine determined him, contrary to his wifhes,
to return, rather than be driven to the neceffity of ftopping half way, or perifhing
with hunger from the difficulty of procuring dogs and provifion.

The wind varied confiderably during my
refidence at Bolcheretfk; it was moft commonly weft, north-weft, or north-eaft; it
blew fometimes from the fouth, but feldom
from

from the eaft. The fouth and weft winds
are almoft invariably attended with fnow.
Scarcely a week paffed, even to the month
of January, without our experiencing two
or three violent tempefts; they commonly
proceeded from the north-weft. Thefe gales
of wind lafted always a day or two, and fometimes feven or eight days. It would have been
the height of imprudence to venture out at
fuch a feafon. The fky was completely
obfcured, and the fnow, fupported by thefe
whirlwinds, formed in the air a thick fog,
that prevented us from feeing at the diftance of fix yards. Woe to all travellers
who are expofed to this terrible weather!
neceffity compels them to ftop, or they run
the rifk of lofing themfelves, or of falling
every moment into fome abyfs; for how is
it poffible they fhould find their way, or
advance a ftep, when they have to refift
the impetuofity of the wind, and to dif-
engage themfelves from the heaps of fnow

L 3   that

that fuddenly encompafs them? If fuch be the dangers encountered by the men, what muft we fuppofe the poor dogs to fuffer. Nothing is more common, when overtaken by thefe hurricanes, than to find ourfelves feparated from the fledges of our companions, to the diftance of two werfts or upwards from each other, and proceeding in an oppofite direction *.

The frequency of thefe tempefts, and the deplorable accidents they occafion, convinced us of the neceffity of deferring our departure. M. Kafloff was equally as impatient to arrive at the place of his deftination, as I was to continue my journey, that I might execute my commiffion with the diligence that had been recommended to me; but every one whofe advice we afked, condemned our eagernefs, and proved par-

* Thefe hurricanes prevail chiefly in the months of November, December, and January.

ticularly

ticularly as to myfelf, that, entrufted with
fuch important difpatches, it would be
rafhnefs to proceed. This reflection paci-
fied me. M. Kafloff anticipated my wifhes,
by giving me a certificate, accounting for
my long refidence at Bolcheretfk, by a re-
lation of the circumftances that had occafioned it. The gales of wind having at
length ceafed towards the middle of January, we eagerly fet about preparing for
our departure, which was fixed for the 27
of that month.

We furnifhed ourfelves in the beft manner we could with brandy, beef, rye, flour,
and oat-meal. A confiderable quantity of
loaves were prepared for us, of which we
referved fome to fupply us during the firft
few days of our journey, and the reft were
cut into thin flices and baked in an oven
like bifcuits: what was left of our flour, we
put into facks as a refource in time of need.

L 4 Mr.

M. Kafloff had ordered that as many
dogs as poffible fhould be collected. Mul-
titudes were prefently brought from all the
neighbouring oftrogs; we had alfo provifion for them in abundance, the only difficulty was how we fhould carry it. We
had refolved to fet off early in the morning of 27; but when we came to load
our fledges, we found our baggage fo
confiderable, that, in fpite of the number
of hands employed, it was not completed
till the evening. We were out of humour;
no day in my life ever appeared fo tedious.
Vexed at the delay, we would not defer our
departure till the next day, and were no
fooner informed that every thing was ready, than we ran to our fledges and were
out of Bolcheretfk in a moment.

We ftarted at feven o'clock. It was moon-
light, and the fnow added to its brightnefs.
Our departure merits a defcription. Conceive

ceive of our numerous cavalcade amounting to thirty-five fledges*. In the firft was
a fergeant of the name of Kabechoff, who
was appointed to fuperintend and direct
our proceffion. He gave the fignal, and
inftantly all thefe fledges fet off in file.
They were drawn by three hundred dogs †
of equal courage and fpeed. Prefently the
line was broken, the order difturbed, and
all was confufion. A fpirited emulation
animated the conductors, and it became as
it were a chariot race. It was who fhould
drive fafteft; no one was willing to be out-
ftripped; the dogs themfelves could not
bear this affront; they partook the rivalfhip

* They were chiefly common fledges, fuch as we have
already defcribed, page 118. Some were clofed in the
manner of *vezocks* or *kibicks*; mine was of this defcription,
as I have mentioned, page 127. In the thirty-five fledges
do not include thofe of the inhabitants of Bolcheretfk, who
accompanied us as far as Apatchin.

† Forty-five dogs were harneffed to M. Kafloff's fledge,
and thirty-feven to mine.

of

of their mafters, fought with one another
to obtain the precedence, and the fledges
were overturned, frequently at the rifk of
being dafhed to pieces. The clamour of
thofe who were overturned, the yelping of
the ftruggling dogs, the mixed cry of thofe
that proceeded, and the confufed and continual chattering of the guides, compleated
the diforder, and prevented us both from
knowing and hearing one another.

To enjoy this tumult the more at my eafe,
I quitted my fledge where I was imprifon-
ed, and placed myfelf in a fmaller one; in
which, befide the pleafure of driving myfelf,
I could fee what was paffing around me.
Fortunately no accident happened, and I
had no reafon to repent of my curiofity.
This embaraffment was chiefly occafioned
by the concourfe of the inhabitants of Bolcheretfk, who, from attachment as well as
refpect, were defirous of accompanying M.
Kafloff

Kafloff to Apatchin*, where we arrived about midnight: the diftance of Bolcheretfk from this oftrog is forty-four werfts.

A few moments after our arrival a tempef- tuous wind arofe, which would greatly have incommoded us, if it had happened during our route. It continued the reft of the night and all the next day, which we were ob- liged therefore to fpend at Apatchin.

Here we received the laft adieux of the inhabitants of Bolcheretfk. I was ftruck with their gratitude and attachment to M. Kafloff, and the regret they expreffed at leaving him, as well as their concern for me, and the intereft they took in the fuccefs of my journey. I was the more pleafed with their attentions, as I had obferved while at Bolcheretfk, that the French nation was not

* I had paffed through this village on my road to Bol- cheretfk, and have defcribed it, page 65.

held

held in any high efteem by them; they had
even fo bad an opinion of us, that it was
with difficulty they were brought to believe what had been told them of the politenefs and cordiality of the crews of the
French frigates to the inhabitants of Saint
Peter and Saint Paul. In proportion how-
evr as they heard their countrymen extol
our conduct, their prejudice grew weaker.
I endeavoured by my converfation and be-
haviour to deftroy it entirely. I dare not
flatter myfelf to have fucceeded ; but it appeared to me that a complete change at laft
took place in their fentiments refpecting us.

The difadvantageous impreffion which
they had imbibed of the character and genius of our nation, originated in the perfidy
and cruelty exhibited in the perfon of the
famous Beniowfky in this part of the peninfula. This flave called himfelf a Frenchman, and acted like a true Vandal.

His

His hiftory is known. During the trou-
bles of 1769 he ferved in Poland under the
colours of the confederates. His intrepidity
induced them to make choice of him to command a medley troop of foreigners, or rather
robbers, like himfelf, whom they kept in
pay, not from choice but neceffity. With
Beniowfky at their head, they ranfacked the
country, maffacring every one they met.
He haraffed the Ruffians, to whom he was as
formidable as to his own countrymen. They
foon felt the neceffity of getting rid of fo
dangerous an enemy: he was taken prifoner,
and it may be fuppofed they adopted no
very lenient meafures refpecting him. Banifhed to Siberia, and afterwards to Kamtfchatka, his fiery and vindictive genius accompanied him. Efcaped from the mountains of fnow, under which the Ruffians fuppofed him to be buried, he fuddenly made
his appearance at Bolcheretfk with a troop
of exiles, to whom he had imparted a fpark

of

of his own audacity. He furprifed the garrifon and took poffeffion of the arms; the
governor, M. Nilloff, was killed by his
hand. There was a veffel in the port; he
feized it: every one trembled at his afpect;
all fubmitted to his will. He compelled the
poor Kamtfchadales to furnifh him with the
provifions he demanded; and not content
with the facrifices obtained, he gave up their
habitations to the unbridled licentioufnefs
of his banditti, to whom he fet the example
of villainy and ferocity. He embarked at
length with his companions, and failed, it
was faid, towards China, carrying with him
the execrations of the people of Kamtfchatka. This fuppofitious Frenchman was the
only one they had yet feen in the peninfula;
and from fuch a fpecimen of our nation,
they certainly could not love, and had fufficient reafon to fear us.

M. Schmaleff quitted us at break of day,
and

and fet off for Tiguil, on the weftern coaft,
to complete the vifit of his government *.

We left Apatchin almoft at the fame time.
Our retinue being lefs numerous we made
more expedition. Having paffed the plain
in which this oftrog is fituated, we met the
Bolchaïa-reka, upon which we journeyed
for feveral hours. We followed it through
all its windings, fometimes in the middle of
a foreft, and fometimes at the foot of fteep
and dreary mountains, which arife at intervals on its banks. Fifteen werfts from
Malkin we left this river, becaufe the current began to put in motion the ice which
was broken in different places; and before
we reached this oftrog, we croffed the Brif-
traïa. We arrived about two o'clock. The
diftance from Apatchin is fixty-four werfts,

* Another object of this journey was to procure us provifions. We rejoined him afterwards, as will be feen in
the fequel.

and

and having no change of dogs, we were
obliged to ftop, to give them time to reft.

The toyon of Malkin came to meet M.
Kafloff, and offered him his ifba. Confiderable preparations had been made for our reception, which induced us to pafs the night
there. He treated us with the utmoft refpect, and entertained us in the beft manner
he could. I regretted that his cares had
not extended to the article of our repofe.
Mine was terribly interrupted by the noife
of our fteeds, to which I was not yet accuftomed. The fhrill and inceffant howlings
of thefe curfed animals, feemed clofe at my
ears, and prevented me from fleeping during
the whole night. It is neceffary to have
heard this nocturnal mufic, the moft difagreeable I ever experienced, to judge of
what I fuffered in habituating myfelf to it;
for in the courfe of my journey I was
obliged to learn to reft in defiance of it.
After

After a few bad nights, fleep at laft over-
powered me, and I was infenfible to all
noife. By degrees I became fo inured to
the cries of thefe animals, that I could repofe in the midft of them in perfect tranquillity. I fhall mention in this place, that
the dogs are only fed once a day, at the end
of their journey ; their repaft confifts commonly of a dried falmon diftributed to each
of them.

The oftrog of Malkin is fimilar to thofe
which I have already defcribed. It contains five or fix ifbas and a dozen balagans,
is fituated upon the border of the Biftraïa,
and furrounded with high mountains. I
had no time to vifit the hot fprings that are
faid to be in this neighbourhood, the waters
of which are ftrongly impregnated with
fulphur; and one in particular, iffuing from
the declivity of a hill, forms at the bottom a
bafon of tolerably clear water.

From Malkin we went to Ganal, which is
forty-five werfts, but we were unable to
travel with the fpeed we had expeƈted.
The Biſtraïa was not completely frozen,
and we were obliged to wind about and to
crofs woods, where the fnow, though deep,
was fo far from firm, that our dogs funk to
their bellies, and were extremely fatigued.
This induced us to abandon this road, and
make again for the Biſtraïa. We came up
to it at ten werfts from Ganal, and found
it in the ſtate we had wifhed. The folidity
of the ice promifed us expeditious travelling, and we readily embraced the advantage. We followed this river till we came
to the oſtrog which is upon its bank, and
confiſts of four iſbas and twelve balagans.
It offered nothing remarkable.

We only learned that there had been
fome very terrible hurricanes, and that they
had not yet fubfided, though their force was

con-

confiderably diminifhed. There is no difficulty in accounting for the violence of
thefe tempefts. The furrounding high
mountains form fo many receffes in which
the wind is embayed. The fewer avenues
it has to efcape at, the more impetuous it
becomes: it feeks out a paffage, rufhes
through the firft that offers, breaks out in
whirlwinds, fcatters the fnow over the roads,
and generally renders them impaffable.

Having fpent a very indifferent night in
the houfe of the toyon of Ganal, we fet off
the next day for Poufchiné. The diftance
is ninety werfts, which however we per-
formed in fourteen hours ; but the laft half
of the journey was very painful. No road
being opened, our fledges funk three or
four feet in the fnow, and the jolts were fo
frequent, that I was happy to efcape with
being only once overturned. We judged
from the fnow upon the trees, that it muft

have

have proceeded from the north, and been very heavy, which was confirmed by the inhabitants. Our road lay invariably through a foreſt of birch trees, and for ſome time we loſt ſight of the mountains, by which we had paſſed the preceding evening; but as we drew nearer to Poufchiné they became viſible again.

The Kamtſchatka runs by the lower end of this oſtrog, which is larger than that of Ganal. The only thing I remarked in this place was, that the iſbas had no chimneys; they have only, like the balagans, a narrow opening in the roof to let out the ſmoak, which is frequently cloſed up by a trap door to confine the heat. It is not poſſible to continue in apartments warmed in this manner; we muſt either come out, or proſtrate ourſelves on the floor, if we would eſcape being ſtifled, or at leaſt blinded, by the ſmoke: it does not aſcend directly towards

wards the roof, but fpreads a thick black
cloud over the chamber ; and as it feldom
has time wholly to evaporate, the interior
part of thefe ifbas is lined with foot, which
gives them a difgufting afpect and a moft
offenfive fmell.

But it is ftill lefs unpleafant than the
noifome odour exhaled from a difmal lamp,
that ferves as a light to the whole houfe.
Its form is not of the moft elegant kind : it
is fimply a hollow pebble or ftone, with a
rag rolled up in the middle for a wick,
round which is placed the greafe of the fea
wolf, or other animals. As foon as the wick
is lighted, we are immediately furrounded
with a dark and thick vapour, which con-
tributes equally with the fmoke to blacken
the whole room: it feifes the nofe and
throat, and penetrates to the very heart.
This is not the only difagreeable fmell that
is experienced in thefe habitations ; there is

M 3 another,

another, in my opinion, much more fetid,
and which I never could endure; it is the
naufeous exhalation from the dried and
ftinking fifh, when it is preparing, when
they are eating it, and even after it is eaten.
The refufe is deftined for the dogs; but before the poor animals get it, every corner
of the room has been fwept with it.

The perfons who inhabit thefe dwellings
exhibit a fpectacle equally difgufting. Here
is a group of women, fhining from the fat
with which they fmear themfelves, and wal-
lowing on the ground amidft a heap of
rags; fome of them fuckling their children, who are half naked, and bedaubed
with filth from head to foot; others devouring with them fome fcraps of fifh perfectly raw, and frequently putrid. There
we fee others in a difhabille that is not lefs
filthy, lying upon bear's fkins, chattering
to one another, and frequently altogether,
and

and employed in various domeſtic occupations, in expectation of their huſbands.

Fortunately the houſes of the toyons
were cleaned as well as poſſible for the reception of M. Kaſloff, who had always the
kindneſs to let me lodge with him.

We ſlept at Pouſchiné in the houſe of the
toyon, and departed very early the next morning ; we only travelled this day thirty four
werſts. It ſeemed that the farther we advanced, the more the roads were obſtructed
with the ſnow. My two conductors were
continually employed in keeping my ſledge
upright, to prevent it from overturning, or
going out of the road ; they were obliged alſo
to exert their lungs to encourage the dogs,
who frequently ſtopped, notwithſtanding the
blows that were beſtowed upon them with
equal profuſion and addreſs. Theſe poor
creatures, whoſe ſtrength is inconceivable,

M 4   had

had all the difficulty in the world to difen-
gage themfelves from the fnow, which covered
them as faft as they fhook it off. It was frequently neceffary to fmooth it before them,
to enable them to extricate the fledge. This
alfo was the office of my guides. To fupport themfelves upon the fnow, they each
faftened a racket to one of their feet, and in
this manner they flid along, refting now and
then their other foot upon the fkate of the
fledge. I doubt whether any exercife can
be more fatiguing, or require greater
ftrength and fkill.

The oftrog of Charom, at which we had
the good fortune to arrive, is fituated upon
the Kamtfchatka : it furnifhed me with no
remarks. We paffed part of the night there,
and left it before day.

In feven hours we reached Vercknei-
Kamtfchatka, which is thirty-five werfts
from

from Charom. Vercknei is a very confiderable place, compared with the oftrogs I had
hitherto feen.   I counted more than a hundred houfes. Its fituation is commodious,
and the profpect round it tolerably various.
Befides bordering upon the river *, it has
the farther advantage of being near to woods
and fields, the foil of which is good, and begins to be cultivated by the inhabitants.
The church is built of wood; its architecture is not difagreeable, and it is only to be
wifhed that the infide correfponded with
the external appearance. The inhabitants
differ in no refpect from thofe of the other
villages. For the firft time I faw at this
place a fpecies of buildings, about the height
of a balagan, that ferve no other purpofe
than to dry fifh. A ferjeant had the command at Vercknei, who lives in a houfe belonging to the crown.

* The Kamtfchatka, which was not yet frozen.

This

This village is alfo the place of refidence
of the unfortunate Ivafchin, whofe hiftory
I related upon my leaving Saint Peter and
Saint Pauls*; he was of our party, and had
only quitted us in order to arrive fooner at
Vercknei, where his firft care had been to
kill one of his oxen, which he entreated us
to accept for our journey, as a teftimony
of his gratitude. This proceeding juftified
the concern I felt for him, whofe afpect
alone made me more than once fhudder at
the idea of his misfortunes. I cannot eafily
conceive how he was able to fupport them,
and reconcile himfelf to his fate: it muft
have been the confcioufnefs of his inno-
cence alone, that could have given him fuch
ftrength of mind. We paid him a vifit
upon our arrival. He was drinking merrily
with fome of his neighbours. His joy was
fincere, and gave us no intimation of a man

* See page 19.

fenfible

fenfible of his paft fufferings, or weary of his prefent fituation.

Our ftay at Vercknei was fhort; we fet out after dinner in order to fleep at Mil-kovaïa-Derevna, otherwife called the village of Milkoff, which was at the diftance of fif-teen werfts. In our way we paffed a tolerably large field inclofed with pallifades, and far-ther on a *zaimka*, that is, a hamlet inhabited by labourers. Thefe labourers were Coffacs, or Ruffian foldiers, employed in the cultivati-on of land on government account. They had eighty horfes belonging to the crown, and which equally anfwer the purpofes of induf-try, and of the ftud eftablifhed in this place for the propagation of animals fo ufeful and fo fcarce in the peninfula. About five hundred yards from this hamlet, which is called Ifchigatchi, upon an arm of the Kamtfchatka, is a water mill built of wood, but not very large. No ufe could at pre-fent

fent be made of it. The fwell of water had
been fo great as to overflow the fluice, and
to fpread itfelf over a part of the plain
where it was frozen. The foil appeared
to be good, and the country round it to be
very pleafant. I queftioned the Coffacs upon
the productions of their canton, where I
conceived every fpecies of corn might be
cultivated with fuccefs. They told me that
their laft harveft had, both in quantity and
quality, furpaffed their hopes, and was not
inferior to the fineft harvefts in Ruffia: two
pouds of corn had produced ten.

Arrived at Milkoff, I was aftonifhed no
longer to fee either Kamtfchadales or Coffacs, but an interefting colony of peafants
whofe features and addrefs told me they
were not a mixed breed. This colony was
felected in 1743, partly in Ruffia and partly
in Siberia, among the primitive inhabitants,
that is, among the hufbandmen. The view
of

of adminiftration, in fending them into this
country was, that they might clear the
land and make experiments in agriculture;
hoping that their example and fuccefs would
inftruct and encourage the indigenes, and
induce them to employ their labours in this
advantageous and neceffary art. Unfortunately their extreme indolence, which I
have already defcribed, little correfponded
with the wife intentions of government;
and fo far are they from pretending to any
rivalfhip, that they have never derived the
fmalleft advantage from the examples that
are before their eyes. This extreme flug-
gifhnefs of the natives is the more painful
to an obferver, as he cannot but admire the
induftry of thefe active emigrants, whofe
labours have been attended with fuch beneficial effects. Their habitations, fituated
upon the Kamtfchatka, feem to fhew that
they live at their eafe. Their cattle thrive
well from the great care they take of them.

I obferved

I obſerved alſo that theſe peaſants had in
general very much the air of being contented with their ſituation. Their labour is
profitable, and not exceſſive. Every man
plows and ſows his field, and having only
his capitation to pay, he reaps abundantly
the fruit of his exertions, which a fertile
ſoil repays him with uſury. I am convinced that greater advantages might be derived from this ſource, if the cultivators
were more numerous. The harveſt conſiſts
chiefly of rye, and a very ſmall quantity of
barley. This colony has nothing to do
with the chace. Government extended its
cares ſo far as to prohibit it, that their
labours might be wholly devoted to agriculture, and that nothing might divert their
attention. The prohibition however, I could
perceive, is not very ſcrupulouſly obſerved.
Their chief is a _ſtaroſte_, appointed by admi-
niſtration, and ſelected from the old men of
the village, as the name implies. His buſineſs

neſs is to inſpect the progreſs of agriculture; to preſide over their ſeed time and
their harveſt, to fix the preciſe period when
they are to take place; in ſhort, to ſtimu-
late the negligence, or encourage the zeal
of the labourers, and particularly to maintain the ſpirit of the eſtabliſhment and a
good underſtanding among them.

Being deſirous of going to Machoure, to
ſpend a day with the baron de Steinheil, I
left M. Kaſloff at Milkoff, and ſet out twenty
four hours before him, that I might occaſion
no delay in his journey. To travel with
the greater expedition I made uſe of a ſmall
ſledge. The roads were no better or leſs
obſtructed with ſnow than what we had
before experienced, and I was therefore unable to make the ſpeed I intended, notwithſtanding my precaution. The firſt village I came to was Kirgan. Before I
reached it, I paſſed a number of houſes and
balagans

balagans that appeared to be deferted, but
I was informed that the fummer regularly
brought back every year their proprietors.
The few habitations which compofe the
oftrog of Kirgan, are built upon the
border of a river called Kirganik, which
is formed by a variety of ftreams that iffue
from then eighbouring mountains, and
unite above the oftrog, fifteen werfts from
Milkoff.

The cold was fo fevere, that notwithftanding the precaution I took of covering
my face with a handkerchief, my cheeks
were frozen in lefs than half an hour. I
had recourfe to the ufual remedy, that of
rubbing my face with fnow, and was relieved at the expence of an acute pain that
continued for feveral days. Though my
face was thus frozen, the reft of my body
experienced the contrary effect. I conducted my own fledge ; and the continual
motion

motion which this exercife requires, added
to the weight of my Kamtfchadale drefs,
threw me into a violent perfpiration, and
fatigued me extremely.

My drefs merits a particular defcription;
by which it will be feen that it gave me no
very alert appearance. Commonly I wore
merely a fimple parque of deers fkin, and
a fur cap, which upon occafion would cover
my ears and part of my cheeks. When the
cold was more piercing, I added to my drefs
two *kouklanki,* a kind of parque that was
larger and made of thicker fkin; one of
them had the hair on the infide, and the
other on the outfide. In the fevereft weather, I put on over all this, another kouklanki, ftill thicker, made of argali, or dogs
fkin, the hairy fide of which is always
undermoft, and the leather or external furface of the fkin painted red. To thefe

kouk-

kouklankis a fmall bib is fixed before, fo
as to guard the face againft the wind : they
have alfo hoods behind, which fall upon the
fhoulders. Sometimes thefe three hoods, one
upon another, compofed my head drefs, by
being drawn over my common cap. My
neck was defended by a cravat called ochei-
nik, made of fable, or the tail of a fox,
and my chin with a chin-cloth made in
like manner of fable, and faftened upon my
head. As the forehead is very fufceptible
of cold, it was covered with an otter or fable fillet, and this was covered again by
my cap. My fur breeches gave me more
warmth than all the reft of my drefs, com-
plicated as it was. I had double deer-fkin
fpatterdafhes, with hair on both fides, and
which are called in Kamtfchatka *tchigi*. I
then put my legs into boots made of deers
fkins, the feet having an interior fole of
tounchitcha, a very foft grafs, which has the
quality of preferving heat. Notwithftanding

ing thefe precautions, my feet, after travelling two or three hours, were very wet,
either from perfpiration or the gradual
penetration of the fnow; and if I ftood
ftill for a moment in my fledge, they be
came immediately frozen. At night I took
off thefe fpatterdafhes, and put on a large
pair of fur ftockings made of deer or argali fkin, and called *ounti*.

Notwithftanding my fatigue, I made no
ftop at Kirgan. A few werfts farther on,
I perceived a volcano to the north, which
emitted no flame, but a column of very thick
fmoke afcended from it. I fhall have occafion to return this way, and will then
fpeak of it more at large. I obferved near
Machoure a wood of firs, tolerably bufhy,
and which was the firft I had feen in Kamtfchatka. The trees were ftrait, but very
flender. At two o'clock in the afternoon I
entered the village of Machoure, which is

N 2   upon

upon the Kamtfchatka, and thirty-feven
werfts from Kirgan.

I alighted at the baron Stenheil's, formerly *capitan ifpravnick,* or infpector of Kamtfchatka, an office afterwards conferred on
M. Schmaleff. Our acquaintance had commenced at Bolcheretfk. I was delighted to
be able to converfe with him in feveral languages, particularly that of my own country, though it was not very familiar to him;
but it was French, and I conceived him to
be my countryman. Whoever has quitted
Europe to travel in fo diftant a part of the
world muft have had fimilar feelings. We
confider every man as a fellow-citizen who
belongs to the fame continent, or fpeaks the
fame language. The moft trivial circum-
flance that reminds us of our country, is
productive of a very fenfible pleafure ; the
heart is eagerly drawn towards the friend,
the brother, whom we conceive we have
found,

found, and feels an inftant defire to repofe
in him all its confidence. The fight of M.
Steinheil imparted to me this delicious fenfa-
tion. There was in his converfation, from
the very firft moment, an irrefiftible attraction. I felt a fort of craving to fee him,
to talk with him; it had the effect of a
charm, though his French, as I have faid,
was not the moft pure, and was pronounced
with the German accent. I fpent the day
of 4 February with the baron, and in the
evening M. Kafloff arrived as he had previoufly informed me.

The oftrog of Machoure, before the in-
troduction of the fmall-pox, was one of the
moft confiderable in the peninfula; but the
ravages of this cruel difeafe, have reduced
the number of inhabitants to twenty families.

All the Kamtfchadales of this village,
N 3   men

men and women, are chamans, or believers
in the witchcraft of thefe pretended forcerers. They dread to an excefs the popes or
Ruffian priefts, for whom they entertain
the moft inveterate hatred. They do all
they can to avoid meeting them. This is
fometimes impoffible, and in that cafe, when
they find them at hand they act the hypocrite, and make their efcape the firft opportunity that offers. I attribute this fear
to the ardent zeal which thefe priefts have
doubtlefs fhown for the extirpation of
idolatry, and which the Kamtfchadales confider as perfecution. They accordingly
look upon them as their greateft enemies.
Perhaps they have reafon to believe, that in
wifhing to convert them, the overthrow of
their idols was not the only thing thefe
miffionaries had in view. Thefe popes probably fet them no example of the virtues
upon which they declaim. It is fufpected
that their object is the acquifiton of wealth,

rather

rather than of profelytes, and the gratification of their inordinate propenfity to
drunkennefs. It is not therefore to be won-
dered at that the inhabitants retain their
ancient errors. They pay a fecret homage
to their god *Koutka**, and place in him fo
entire a confidence, that they addrefs their
prayers exclufively to him when they are
defirous of obtaining any boon, or of en-
gaging in any enterprife. When they go
to the chace, they abftain from wafhing
themfelves, and are careful not to make the
fign of the crofs : they invoke their Koutka,
and the firft animal they catch is immediately facrificed to him. After this act
of devotion they conceive that their chace
will be fuccefsful; on the contrary, if
they were to crofs themfelves, they would
defpair of catching any thing. It is alfo a
part of their fuperftition to confecrate to

---

* This object of their worfhip is accurately defcribed
in Steller.

Koutka

Koutka their new-born children, who, the moment they have left their cradle, are deftined to become chamans. The veneration of the inhabitants of this village for forcecerers can fcarcely be conceived; it approaches to infanity, and is really to be pitied; for the extravagant and wild abfurdities by which thefe magicians keep alive the credulity of their compatriots, excites our indignation rather than our laughter. At prefent they do not profefs their art openly, or give the fame fplendour they once did to their necromancy. They no longer decorate their garments with myftic rings and other fymbolic figures of metal, that jingled together upon the flighteft motion of their body. In like manner they have abandoned the kind of kettle *, which they ufed to ftrike with a fort of mufical intonation in their pretended en-

* A fort of *tambour de vafque* called *bouben.* It is ftill in ufe amongft the Yakoutfk, as will be feen hereafter.

chantments,

chantments, and with which they announc-
ed their approach. In fhort, they have for-
faken all their magic inftruments. The
following are the ceremonies they obferve
in their affemblies, which they are careful
to hold in fecret, though not the lefs frequently on that account. Conceive of a
circle of fpeftators, ftupidly rapt in attention and ranged round the magician, male
or female, for as I have before obferved, the
women are equally initiated into the myf-
teries. All at once he begins to fing, or to
utter fhrill founds without either meafure or
fignification. The docile affembly ftrike
in with him, and the concert becomes a
medley of harfh and infupportable difcords.
By degrees the chaman is warmed, and he
begins to dance to the confufed accents of
his auditory, who become hoarfe and exhaufted from the violence of their exertions. As the prophetic fpirit is excited
in the minifter of their Koutka, the ani-
mation

mation of the dance increafes. Like the
Pythian on the tripos, he rolls his ghaftly
and haggard eyes ; all his motions are convulfive; his mouth is drawn awry, his limbs
ftiffened, and every diftortion and grimace
is put in practice by him, to the great admiration of his difciples. Having acted
thefe buffooneries for fome time, he fuddenly ftops, as if infpired, and becomes
now as compofed as he was before agitated. It is the facred collectednefs of a man
full of the god that governs him, and who
is about to fpeak by his voice. Surprifed
and trembling, the affembly is inftantly
mute, in expectation of the marvels that
are to be revealed. The felf-created pro-
phet then utters at different intervals,
broken fentences, words without meaning,
and what ever nonfenfe comes into the
head of the impoftor ; and this is invariably confidered as the effect of infpiration.
His jargon is accompanied either with a

torrent

torrent of tears or loud burfts of laughter,
according to the complexion of the tidings
he has to announce ; and the expreffion and
gefture of the orator vary in conformity to
his feelings. I was furnifhed with this account by perfons entitled to credit, and who
had contrived to be prefent at thefe abfurd
revelations.

There feems to be fome analogy between
thefe chamans, and the fect called quakers.
The quakers pretend equally to infpiration,
and there are individuls among them, who,
guided by its fuppofed impulfe, hold forth
in their filent meetings, and break out in
piteous lamentations, or fudden ftarts of
extravagant joy. The difference is this:
thefe prompt orators harangue extempore
upon the fubject of morality, whofe funda-
mental principles they endeavour to re-
commend ; whereas the Kamtfchadale de-
claimers underftand not a word of what
they

they utter, and only make ufe of their my-
fterious and hypocritical jargon to increafe
the idolatry of their ftupid admirers.

At Machoure the intelligence which M.
Kafloff had before received from Bogenoff,
an engineer, was confirmed. He had been
fent along the river Pengina to fix upon a
fituation for a town, and trace the plan of
it, with directions to proceed afterwards by
the weftern coaft of Kamtfchatka as far as
Tiguil, and make an exact map of the country as he paffed. On his arrival at Kaminoi *, he told M. Kafloff that he had met
a confiderable number of revolted Koriacs,
who came out to intercept his paffage, and
prevent him from executing his miffion. It
was now added to the account, that they
amounted to a body of fix hundred men,
and that we fhould not probably be per-

* A village upon the border of the river Pengina.

mitted

mitted to advance. This was melancholy news, for me particularly, who longed to arrive at Okotfk, as if it had been the end of my journey, or as if I could thence reach France in a fingle day. How diftreffing the thought, that there was no other way but through this village, and that I fhould perhaps be obliged to turn back! My impatience made me fhudder at the very idea. M. Kafloff participated my feelings, and was of opinion with me that the report ought not to ftop us. It might not be accurate; the narrators might have given it an air of importance, to which it was not entitled; their fears might have magnified it; and each perhaps had made fome addition to the ftory. Thefe confiderations led us to doubt, and we refolved to fatisfy ourfelves in perfon of its truth, thinking it time enough to have recourfe to expedients if the rebels were actually to oppofe our paffage. We were prefently encouraged by the

the arrival of an exprefs to M. Kafloff, who
had met with no interruption, and who affured us that every thing had the appearance of perfect tranquillity.

At break of day I took leave of the baron
de Steinheil, with equal regret and gratitude
for his kind reception, and the attentions he
had paid me during my fhort vifit. His
information and accomplifhments rendered
him a truly interefting character *.

We

* I had the misfortune, while at Machoure, to lofe the
fable M. Kafloff had given me, which died in fpite of all
the cares I took of it. I preferved however the fkin. It
had been a confiderable amufement to me to obferve its
motions. Its extreme activity rendered its chain infupportable. It frequently attempted to efcape, and would infallibly have fucceeded, if I had not watched it continually ;
and I never caught it again without experiencing the
marks of its teeth. It fed upon fifh and meat ; the latter
was preferred, and is the favourite food of thefe animals in
their wild ftate. Their addrefs in catching birds and animals inferior to themfelves, is aftonifhing. Mine flept almoft all day, and made a continual racket in the night by
fhaking its chain ; but timid to excefs, it ceafed to make
the

We travelled this day fixty-fix werfts upon the Kamtfchatka, the ice of which was very firm and perfectly fmooth. I faw nothing remarkable in my way, nor in the village of Chapina, where we arrived at fun-fet.

We fat off early the next morning, and found the fnow very troublefome. It was fo thick upon the ground, that we were fcarcely able to go on. We journeyed all the day though very thick woods of fir and birch trees. About half-way, and again farther on, we met two rivers, one of which was very fmall, and the other fixty yards wide; it is called the great Ni-koulka. They are both formed by ftreams

the leaft noife when it faw any one coming, and began again the moment it was alone. I ufed to let it out feve-ral times a day, and as foon as it was upon the fnow, it began to burrow and conceal itfelf under it like a mole, appearing every now and then, and hiding itfelf again immediately.

iffuing

iffuing from the mountains, and uniting at
this place to pay their tribute together to the
Kamtfchatka. Neither of them was frozen,
which I afcribed to the extreme rapidity of
their current. The fpot where we paffed them
was truly pi&turefque ; but the moft fingular obje&t was the numerous firs that fkirted
thefe rivers, and which feemed like fo many
trees of ice. A thick hoar-froft, occafioned
perhaps by the dampnefs of the place, covered every branch, and gave to the whole
a bright and chryftalline appearance.

At fome diftance from Tolbatchina we
croffed a heath, from which I could perceive three volcanos ; none of them threw
up any flames, but merely clouds of very
black fmoke. The firft, which I before
mentioned in going to Machoure, has its
refervoir in the bowels of a mountain that
is not exa&tly of a conical fhape, the fummit being flattened and but little elevated.
                                        This

This volcano, I was informed, had been at
reſt for ſome time, and was ſuppoſed to be
extinguiſhed, but it had lately kindled
again. North-eaſt of this is a peak, the
top of which appears to be the crater of
a ſecond volcano, which continually throws
up ſmoke, though I could not perceive the
ſmalleſt ſpark of fire. The third is north-
north-eaſt of the ſecond; I could not obſerve it as I wiſhed, a high mountain inter-
cepting almoſt entirely my view. It de-
rives its name from the village of Klutchef-
ſkaïa, near which it is ſituated; and I was
told that we ſhould paſs cloſer to it hereafter. The two other volcanos are called
in like manner after the oſtrog of Tolbatchina, where we arrived in good time. This
village is upon the Kamtſchatka, forty-four
werſts from Chapina, but it contains nothing extraordinary. We were informed
that there had been a Kamtſchadale wedding in the morning. I regretted the not

O having

having been prefent at this ceremony, which, as I was told, is nearly the fame as in Ruffia. I faw the new married couple, who appeared to be two children. I afked their age. The bridegroom was but fourteen, and the bride only eleven. Such marriages would be confidered as premature in any country except Afia.

I had an extreme defire to fee the town of Nijenei-Kamtfchatka, and had long thought how to fatisfy it ; to have left the peninfula without vifiting the capital, I fhould have confidered as an unpardonable fault. My curiofity did not interfere with my refolution of travelling with all poffible expedition. I was obliged indeed to make a circuit, but it was not fo far as to occafion a delay of any confequence. Having concerted with M. Kafloff, who was anxious to procure every thing that could render my journey agreeable and fafe, I engaged

to

to join him at the village of Yelofki, where
the arrangement of fome affairs of his government would detain him feveral days.

That I might lofe lefs time, I took leave
of him the evening of our arrival at Tolbatchina. But the roads were ftill worfe
than any we had yet met with. It was
with the utmoft difficulty I could reach
Kofirefski by break of day, a village fixty-fix
werfts from Tolbatchina.

I made no ftay, elated with having happily efcaped all the dangers that befet me
in fo terrible a road, and in the darknefs of
the night *. I conceived that I had nothing to fear in the day, and proceeded
with a kind of confidence for which I was

---

* I learned afterwards that the fledge of M. Kalloff,
who paffed at noon day, had barely efcaped from being
dafhed to pieces in running againft a tree, and that two of
his conductors had been hurt by the violence of the fhock.

foon

foon punifhed. After having travelled a confiderable number of werfts upon the Kamtfchatka, which I had been delighted to find again, and the width of which in this place particularly ftruck me, I was obliged to quit it and enter a fort of ftrait, where the fnow, driven by the hurricanes, prefented an uneven and deceitful furface. It was impoffible to fee or avoid the rocks that furrounded me. I prefently heard a crack that told me my fledge was damaged; it was in reality one of my fkates broken in two. My guides affifted me in adjufting it in the beft manner we could, and we had the good fortune to reach Ouchkoff without any other accident. It was midnight, and we travelled this day fixty-fix werfts. My firft care was to refit my fledge, which detained me till the next day.

There are in this village one ifba, and eleven balagans ; the number of inhabitants is

is reduced to five families, who are divided
into three yourts. In the neighbourhood
is a lake which abounds fo much with fifh,
that all the villages round refort to it for
their winter ftock. It is alfo a confiderable refource for the capital, which would
otherwife be almoft deftitute of a provifion
of the firft neceffity throughout the peninfula.

I left Ouchkoff early in the morning, and
at noon had travelled forty-four werfts,
partly upon the Kamtfchatka, and partly
acrofs extenfive heaths. The firft village I
came to was Kreftoff. It was a little larger
than the preceding oftrog, but fimilar in
other refpects to what I had before feen.
I only ftayed to change my dogs. Hitherto
I had purfued the road which M. Kafloff
was to take to get to Yelofki ; but inftead
of proceeding like him to Khartchina, I
directed my courfe, upon coming out of

Kreftoff,

Kreſtoff, towards the village of Klutchefskaïa, which is thirty werſts from it.

The weather, which, ſince our departure
from Apatchin, had been very fine, though
cold, changed all of a ſudden in the afternoon. The ſky became clouded, and the
wind, which roſe in the weſt, brought us
a heavy ſnow. It extremely incommoded
us, and prevented me from examining as I
could have wiſhed, the volcano of Klutchefskaïa, which I had ſeen at the ſame
time with thoſe of Tolbatchina. As far as
I could judge, the mountain that carries it
in its womb, is conſiderably higher than the
other two. It continually throws up flames,
which ſeem to aſcend from the midſt of
the ſnow, with which the mountain is covered to its very ſummit.

Upon the approach of night I came to
the village of Klutchefskaïa. The inhabitants

tants are all Siberian peafants, from the
neighbourhood of the Lena, and were fent
about fifty years ago into this part of the
peninfula to cultivate the land. The number of males, including men and children,
fcarcely exceed fifty. The fmall-pox attacked only thofe who had not before been
affected with it; but it carried off more
than one half of them. Thefe labourers are
lefs happy than thofe who live in the neighbourhood of Verknei-Kamtfchatka. The
quantity and quality of their laft harveft,
both rye and barley, exceeded their hopes.
Thefe peafants have many horfes belonging to them; in the mean time there are
fome which are the property of government.

This oftrog is tolerably large, and appears the more fo from being divided into
two parts, about four hundred yards from
each other. It extends principally from

eaft to weft. To the eaftward is fituated
the church, which is built of wood, and in
the Ruffian tafte. The majority of houfes
are better conftructed, and are more clean,
than any I have yet feen. There are alfo
fome confiderable magazines. The number of balagans is fmall, and they are very
unlike thofe of the Kamtfchadales; their
form is oblong, and their roof, which has
the fame declivity as ours, refts upon pofts,
which fupport it in the air.

The Kamtfchatka paffes at the bottom of
the oftrog; it is never entirely frozen in
this part. In fummer it frequently overflows and enters the very houfes, though
they are all of them built upon an eminence.

Four werfts eaft of the church of Klutchefskaïa, is another *zaimka*, or little hamlet, inhabited by Coffacs or labouring foldiers,

diers, whofe harvefts belong to government: but I cannot get out of my way to
examine it.

I made a very fhort ftay at Klutchef-
fkaïa, my impatience to fee Nijenei induc-
ing me to leave it the fame evening in order to reach Kamini, a Kamtfchadale village, twenty werfts farther. I arrived at
midnight, but merely paffed through it.

Before day I was at Kamokoff, twenty
werfts from Kamini. I foon arrived at
Tchokofskoi, or Tchoka, which is twenty-
two werfts farther. From thence to Nijenei, the diftance is the fame, and I travelled it equally in a few hours. I had the
pleafure of entering a little before noon into this capital of Kamtfchatka, which is feen
at a confiderable diftance, but its appearance
is neither ftriking nor agreeable.

If

It prefents to our view merely a clufter of houfes, with three fteeples rifing above them, and is fituated upon the border of the Kamt-fchatka, in a bafon formed by a chain of mountains that raife their lofty heads around it, but which are however at a tolerable diftance. Such is the pofition of the town of Nijenei, of which I had a higher opinion before I faw it. The houfes, amounting to about a hundred and fifty, are of wood, built in a very bad tafte, fmall, and buried befide under the fnow, which the hurri-canes collect there. Thefe hurricanes pre-vail almoft continually in this quarter, and have only ceafed within a few days. There are two churches at Nijenei, one is in the town, and has two fteeples; the other be-longs to, and is in the circuit of the fort. Thefe two buildings are wretchedly con-ftructed. The fort is almoft in the middle of the town, and is a large palifaded en-clofure of a fquare form. Befides the church, the

the enclofure contains alfo the magazines,
the arfenal, and the guard-houfe: a fentinel
is ftationed at the entrance both day and
night. The houfe of the governor, major
Orleankoff, is near the fortrefs, and, its fize
excepted, is fimilar to the reft of the houfes;
it is neither higher, nor built in a better
tafte.

I alighted at the houfe of an unfortunate
exile, named Snafidoff, who had fuffered
the fame punifhment as Ivafchkin, nearly at
the fame time, but for different caufes : like
Ivafchkin, he had been banifhed to Kamtfchatka ever fince the year 1744.

I had fcarcely entered, when an officer
from M. Orleankoff came to congratulate
me upon my happy arrival. He was followed by many of the principal officers of
the town, who came one after another in
the moft obliging manner to offer me their
fervices.

fervices. I expreffed a becoming fenfe of their civilities, but was mortified at their having taken me by furprife. As foon as I was dreffed, I haftened to return my thanks to each of them feparately. I began with major Orleankoff, whom I found bufily pre-paring for an entertainment that he was to give the next day, upon the marriage of a Pole in the Ruffian fervice, with the niece of the protapope, or chief prieft. He had not only the politenefs to invite me to the wedding, but came to me in the morning, and conducted me to his houfe, that I might lofe no part of this fpectacle, which he rightly judged was calculated to intereft me.

In the mean time what ftruck me moft was the ftrictnefs of the ceremonial. The diftinction of rank feemed to be obferved with the moft fcrupulous delicacy. The formality, compliments, and cold civilities, which

which opened the entertainment, gave it
a ftarched air, that promifed more dulnefs
than gaiety. The repaft was the moft fumptuous the country could furnifh. Among
other difhes there was a variety of foups,
accompanied with cold meats, upon which
we fed heartily. The fecond fervice confifted of roafted difhes and paftry. The
dinner had lefs the appearance of fenfuality
than profufion. The liquors were the produce of the different fruits of the country, boiled up and mixed with French
brandy. But a profufion of the brandy of
the country, made from the *flatkaïa-trava*,
or fweet herb, which I have already noticed,
was almoft continually ferved round in preference. This liquor has no difagreeable
tafte, and is even aromatic; they ufe it the
more readily, as it is lefs unwholefome than
the brandy diftilled from corn. The guefts
by degrees aflumed an air of good humour.
Their heads were not proof againft the
fumes

fumes of fo ftrong a beverage, and foon the groffeft mirth circulated round the table. To this noify and fumptuous feaft a ball fucceeded, that was conducted with tolerable regularity. The company were gay, and amufed themfelves till the evening with Po- lifh and Ruffian country dances. The fef- tival ended with a fplendid fire-work, that had been prepared by M. Orleankoff, and which he himfelf let off. It was only a trifling one, but it had a good effect, and left nothing to be defired. I enjoyed the aftonifhment and extafy of the fpectators, who were little accuftomed to exhibitions of this nature: it was a fubject for a pain- ter. Rapt in admiration, they exclaimed in full chorus at every fquib. The regret they expreffed at its fhort duration afforded me equal amufement. It was neceffary to attend to the extravagant encomiums that were unanimoufly beftowed upon them; and on departing, every individual fighed

over

over the remembrance of all the pleafures
of the day.

The next day I was invited to the houfe
of the protapope, uncle to the bride, where
the entertainment was fimilar to that of the
preceding one, except the fire-work. I have
already obferved, that the protapope is chief
of all the churches in Kamtfchatka. The
clergy throughout the peninfula are fubordinate to him, and he has the decifion of all
ecclefiaftical affairs. His refidence is at Nijenei. He is an old man, not entirely deprived of his vigour, with a long white beard
which flows down upon his breaft and gives
him a truly venerable appearance. His converfation is fenfible, fprightly, and calculated to gain him the refpect and affection of
the people.

There are two tribunals at Nijenei, one
that concerns the governments, and the other
takes

takes cognizance of all mercantile difputes.
The magiftrate who prefides in the latter, is
a kind of burgomafter, fubject to the orders
of the *gorodnitch*, or governor of the town.
We have already feen that each of thefe
jurifdictions holds from the tribunal of
Okotfk, to the governor of which it is accountable for all its proceedings.

But what moft interefted me at Nijenei,
and what I cannot pafs over in filence, was
my finding there nine Japanefe, who had
been brought thither in the preceding fummer, from the Aleutienne iflands, by a Ruffian veffel employed in the trade of otter
fkins.

One of the Japanefe informed me, that
he and his companions had embarked in a
fhip of their own country, with an intention of vifiting the more fouthern Kurilles
iflands, for the purpofe of trading with
the

the inhabitants. They directed their courſe
along the coaſt, and were at a ſmall diſtance
from it, when they were overtaken by a
violent gale, which carried them out to ſea,
and deprived them of all knowledge where
they were. According to his account, which
however I did not altogether believe, they
beat about in the ocean for near ſix months
without ſeeing land; of courſe they muſt
have had a plentiful ſtock of proviſions.
At length they diſcerned the Aleutienne
iſlands, and tranſported with joy, they determined to make for that coaſt, without
well knowing in what part of the world
it was. They accordingly caſt anchor near
one of the iſlands, and a ſmall ſhallop
brought them to land. At this place they
found certain Ruſſians, who propoſed to
them to unlade their veſſel, and remove it
to a place of ſecurity; but either from ſuſ-
picion, or perhaps that they thought the
next day would be early enough, the Japa-

neſe

nefe peremptorily refufed. They had foon occafion to repent of their negligence. That very night there arofe a ftrong gale, during which their fhip ftranded ; and as this was not difcovered till break of day, they had the utmoft difficulty to fave a fmall part of the cargo, and fome pieces of the veffel, which had been almoft entirely conftructed of cedar. The Ruffians, who had before treated them with civility, now exerted every effort in their power to make thefe unfortunate people forget their lofs. They at length perfuaded them to accompany them to Kamtfchatka, whither they were bound upon their return. My Japanefe added, that they had at firft been much more numerous, but that the fatigues of the fea, and afterwards the rigour of the climate, had taken off many of his companions.

My informer appeared to have over his eight countrymen a very diftinguifhed fupe-riority ;

riority; and he informed us that he was
himfelf a merchant, and the reft only failors under his command. Certain it is, that
they entertain for him a fingular veneration
and friendfhip. They are penetrated with
grief, and fhew the greateft uneafinefs when
he is indifpofed, or the leaft unfavourable
accident has befallen him. They regularly
fend twice a day one of their body to
wait upon him. His friendfhip for them
may be faid not to be lefs; not a day
paffes without his vifiting them, and he
employs the greateft care that they fhould
be in want of nothing. His name is
Kodaïl: his figure has nothing in it fingular, and is even agreeable; his eyes do
not project like thofe of the Chinefe; his
nofe is long, and he has a beard which he
frequently fhaves. He is about five feet in
ftature, and is tolerably well made. At
firft he wore his hair in the Chinefe fafhion; that is, he had a fingle lock depend-
ing from the middle of his head, the reft

P 2   of

of his hair round it being clofe fhaved; but he has lately been perfuaded to let it grow, and to tie it after the French fafhion. He is extremely apprehenfive of cold, and the warmeft garments given him are fcarcely able to fave him from it. Under thefe he conftantly wears the drefs of his country: this confifts in the firft place of one or more long chemifes of filk, like our dreffing gowns; and over thefe he wears one of woollen, which feems to imply that this fort of materials is more precious in their eftimation than filk. Perhaps however the circumftance arifes from fome motive of con-venience, of which I am ignorant. The fleeves of this garment are long and open; and, in fpite of the rigour of the climate, he has conftantly his arms and his neck un-covered. They put a handkerchief about his neck when he goes abroad, which he takes off as foon as he enters a houfe, being, as he fays, unable to fupport it.

His

His fuperiority over his countrymen was
calculated to make him be diftinguifhed ;
but this circumftance has lefs weight than
the vivacity of his temper and the mildnefs
of his difpofition. He lodges and eats at
the houfe of major Orleankoff. The free-
dom with which he enters the houfe of the
governor and other perfons, would among
us be thought infolent, or at leaft rude.
He immediately fixes himfelf as much at his
eafe as poffible, and takes the firft chair that
offers ; he afks for whatever he wants, or
helps himfelf, if it be within his reach.
He fmokes almoft inceffantly; his pipe is
fhort, and ornamented with filver ; he puts
into it a very fmall quantity of tobacco,
which he renews every moment. To this
habit he is fo much addicted, that it was
with difficulty they could perfuade him to
part with his pipe even at meals. He is
poffeffed of great penetration, and appre-
hends with admirable readinefs every thing

P 3   you

you are defirous to communicate. He has
much curiofity, and is an accurate obferver.
I was affured that he kept a minute journal
of every thing he faw, and all that happened to him. Indeed the objects and the
cuftoms he has an opportunity to obferve,
have fo little refemblance to thofe of his
country, that every thing furnifhes him with
a fubject of remark. Attentive to whatever
paffes, or is faid in his prefence, he puts it
into writing, for fear of forgetting it. His
characters appeared to me confiderably to
refemble the Chinefe, but the form of writing is different, thefe writing from right to
left, and the Japanefe from the top of the
page to the bottom. He fpeaks Ruffian
with fufficient eafe to make himfelf underftood : you muft however be ufed to his
pronunciation to converfe with him, as he
delivers himfelf with a volubility that frequently obliges you to mifs fomething he
fays, or apprehend it in a wrong fenfe. His
repartees

repartees are in general fprightly and natural. He employs no concealment or referve, but tells with the utmoft franknefs
what he thinks of every one. His company
is agreeable, and his temper tolerably even,
though with a confiderable tendency to fuf-
picion. Does he mifs any thing? he inftantly imagines that it has been ftolen from
him, and difcovers anxiety and difquietude.
His fobriety is admirable, and perfectly con-
trafts with the manners of this country.
When he has determined to drink no ftrong
liquor, it is impoffible to induce him fo much
as to tafte it; when he is inclined, he afks
for it of his own accord, but never drinks
to excefs. I obferved alfo, that, after the
manner of the Chinefe, in eating he made
ufe of two little fticks, which he handled
with great dexterity.

I requefted to fee fome of the coin of his
country, and he readily gratified my cu-
P 4   riofity.

riofity. The gold coin was a thin plate of an oval form, and of about two inches in its longeft diameter. It is marked with various Japanefe chara&ters, and it appeared to be of pure gold, without any alloy, fo that it readily bent in any manner you pleafed. Their filver money is fquare, fmaller, thinner, and lighter than that of gold; he however affured me that at Japan this was the fuperior coin. The copper coin is precifely the fame as the *cache* of the Chinefe: it is round, and nearly of the fize of our two *liard* pieces, with a fquare perforation in the middle.

I afked him fome queftions refpecting the nature of the merchandize they had faved from their wreck, and I underftood, from his anfwer, that it confifted chiefly in cups, plates, boxes, and other commodities of that fort, with a very fine varnifh. I
after-

afterwards found they had fold a part of them at Kamtfchatka.

I truft I fhall be forgiven this digreffion upon thefe Japanefe; I can fcarcely imagine that it will be thought impertinent; it will affift us in becoming acquainted with a nation that we have fcarcely an opportunity to fee and obferve.

Having fpent three days at Nijenei Kamtfchatka, I left it 12 February at one o'clock in the afternoon, to meet M. Kafloff, whom I was fure of finding at Yelofki. My road for fome time was the fame as I had already travelled in going to Nijenei, and I arrived at Tchoka early in the evening. A ftrong wefterly wind almoft always prevails in this place. The fituation of the oftrog fufficiently accounts for it, which is upon a river that runs between two chains of
mountains

mountains that ftretch along its banks to the diftance of twenty five werfts.

I paffed the night at Kamokoff, and the next morning I arrived in a few hours at the oftrog of Kamini, or Peter's town, where I took the road to Kartchina. In my way I paffed three lakes, the laft of which was very large, and not lefs than five leagues in circumference. I flept at this oftrog, which is forty werfts from the preceding one, and fituated upon the river Kartchina *.

I fet off as foon as it was light, and not-withftanding the bad weather, which lafted all the day, I travelled feventy werfts, which brought me to Yelofki. It is upon a river of the fame name, and furrounded with mountains.

* The villages have almoft univerfally the fame name as the rivers upon which they are placed, thofe only excepted which are upon the Kamtfchatka.

M. Kafloff

M. Kaſloff was aſtoniſhed at my expedition. I had vainly flattered myſelf, that the
moment of our meeting would be that of
our departure ; but his buſineſs was not
yet finiſhed, and we were obliged to prolong our ſtay: he hoped alſo that M.
Schmaleff would ſoon arrive. We had calculated that he would meet us at this oſtrog.
This expectation, which was fruitleſs, and
the affairs of M. Kaſloff, detained us five
days longer. At length he complied with
my impatience, and agreed to ſet off the
19, very early in the morning.

We travelled fifty four werſts gently
enough ; but in the afternoon we were ſuddenly overtaken by a terrible tempeſt from
the weſt and north-weſt. We were in an
open country, and the whirlwinds became
ſo violent, that it was impoſſible to proceed.
The ſnow, which they raiſed in the air at
every blaſt, formed a thick fog, and our
guides,

guides, notwithftanding their knowledge of
the roads, could no longer be anfwerable
for not mifleading us. We could not pre-
vail on them to conduct us any farther:
and yet it was dreadful to lie to at the
mercy of fo impetuous a hurricane. As to
myfelf, I confefs that I began to fuffer extremely, when our guides propofed to lead
us to a wood that was not far off, and where
we fhould at leaft find fome kind of fhelter.
We hefitated not a moment to avail ourfelves of their civility; but before we quitted the road, it was neceffary to wait till
our fledges could be affembled, or we fhould
otherwife run the rifk of being feparated
from one another, and entirely loft. Having effected this, we gained the wood, which
was happily at the diftance that we had
been informed. Our halt took place about
two o'clock in the afternoon.

The firft care of our Kamtfchadales was
to

to dig a hole in the fnow, which was in this place at leaft fix feet deep; others fetched wood, and a fire being quickly lighted, the kettle was fet on. A light repaft, and a fmall dram of brandy, foon recovered all our company. As the night approached, we were employed upon the means of pafsing it in the leaft uncomfortable manner. Each prepared his own bed: mine was my vezock, where I could lie down at my eafe; but except M. Kafloff, there was no other perfon who had fo convenient a carriage. How, faid I to myfelf, will thefe poor creatures contrive to fleep? I was foon relieved from my anxiety on their account. The manner in which they prepared their beds, deferves to be mentioned, though they did not obferve much ceremony on the occafion. Having dug a hole in the fnow, they covered it with the branches of trees, the fmalleft they could get; then wrapping themfelves up in a *kouklanki*, with the hood drawn over

their

their heads, they lay down on their bed as if
it were the beſt in the world. As to our dogs,
they were unharneſſed, and tied to the trees
that were near us, where they paſſed the
night in their uſual manner.

The wind having conſiderably abated,
we proceeded on our journey before it was
light. We had thirty werſts to Ozernoï,
where it had been our intention to have
ſlept the preceding evening. We arrived
at ten o'clock in the morning, but our dogs
being extremely fatigued, we were obliged
to ſpend the reſt of the day, and even the
night there, in hopes that the wind, which
began to blow ſtill more violently in the
afternoon, would ſubſide during the interval.

The oſtrog takes its name from a lake
that is near it. The river Ozernaïa, which
is but ſmall, runs at the bottom of the village.

lage. The houfe of the toyon was the only
ifba I faw, and I was informed that we
fhould meet with no more of thefe kind of
buildings till we came to the town of Ingiga.
There were, however, fifteen balagans and
two yourts. I might here defcribe thefe
fubterraneous habitations; but as they are
fmall in comparifon with thofe which I fhall
foon have an opportunity of examining, I
fhall defer my defcription for the prefent.

We paffed alfo the 21 February at Ozer-
noï, in fruitlefs expectation of a ferjeant of
M. Kafloff's fuite, who had been fent to
Nijenei-Kamtfchatka.

The next day we reached Ouké at a
tolerably early hour, which is only twenty
fix werfts. There we waited again for the
ferjeant, who had been ordered to join us at
this place. But he did not come.

There

There is but one iſba at Ouké, which, together with a dozen balagans and two yourts, form the whole oſtrog. One of the yourts had been cleaned for M. Kaſloff, and we paſſed the night in it.

We left this village at break of day, and half way on our journey we ſaw a certain number of balagans, which are only inhabited, I was informed, in the fiſhing ſeaſon. Near this place we met the ſea again, and travelled on the ſhore for ſome time. I was extremely mortified at not being able to ſee at what diſtance it was frozen, nor what was the direction of this part of the eaſtern coaſt of Kamtſchatka. A north wind incommoded us, and impelled the ſnow with ſuch violence againſt us, that our whole attention was engroſſed by guarding our eyes from it; there was alſo a fog that extended from the ſhore to a conſiderable diſtance on the ſea, and intercepted almoſt

entirely

entirely the view of it. The inhabitants of
the country, whom I interrogated upon the
fubject, informed me we had juft paffed
a bay of no very confiderable width, and
that the fea was covered with ice as far as
thirty werfts from the land.

At Khaluli, an oftrog, fituated upon a
river of the fame name, fixty fix werfts
from Ouké, and at a fhort diftance from the
fea, I found but two yourts and twelve or
thirteen balagans; but I had the pleafure
of feeing a baidar covered with leather.
This boat was about fifteen feet long and
four wide; the hull was made of planks
tolerably thin, and croffing each other; a
longer and thicker piece of wood ferved as
the keel; the timbers were made faft with
leathern ftraps; and the whole was covered
over with feveral fkins of fea horfes and
large fea wolves.

I particularly admired the manner in
which thefe fkins were prepared, and the
compactnefs with which they were fewn
together, fo that the water could not penetrate into the boat. Its fhape was fomewhat fimilar to ours, but lefs round, and
therefore lefs graceful; it converged towards the extremities, fo as to terminate in
a point, and had a flat bottom. The lightnefs of the common baidars, which makes
them liable to be overturned, doubtlefs
gave rife to this mode of conftructing them,
by which they acquire more weight. This
boat was placed under a fhed built on purpofe to protect it from the fnow. The
toyon of Khaluli having given up his yourt
to us, we flept in it, being unable to proceed till the next day. The wind had increafed fince our arrival, and did not abate
till the middle of the night.

At ten o'clock in the morning we had loft
fight

fight of Khaluli, and paffed an old village
of the fame name, which had been lately
deferted on account of its bad fituation.
Farther on we found fome more defolated
habitations, formerly the oftrog of Ivafchkin,
and which had been removed, for a fimilar
reafon, thirty werfts from its former fituation. We came again to the fea, and travelled for fome time on the eaftern coaft.
It forms another bay at this place, which I
was defirous of examining, but was, as before, prevented by the fog. I obferved that
the fog cleared up in proportion as the
wind veered to the noith-eaft, which had
hitherto been weft and north-weft.

Ivafchkin is forty werfts from Khaluli,
and very near to the fea. It contains two
yourts and fix balagans, and is fituated
upon a fmall river of the fame name, which
was entirely frozen, as was alfo one that we
had juft paffed.

Q 2   We

We flept at this village, and fpent a confiderable part of the next day there, from
the apprehenfion of a hurricane, which, it
was faid, threatened us. We were at laft
relieved from our fears, and though it was
tolerably late when we refolved to proceed,
we reached Drannki, which is thirty werfts.
The fituation of this oftrog is fimilar to the
preceding one. Here we found M. Haus,
a Ruffian officer: he came from Tiguil, and
brought M. Kafloff various objects of natural hiftory.

We left Drannki at break of day. In
the afternoon we croffed a bay that was
fifteen werfts wide, and from twenty-five to
thirty deep ; the entrance was fcarcely lefs
than five werfts : it is formed by the fouth
coaft. This coaft is low land, gradually
declining as it advances into the fea. The
bay runs weft-north-weft and eaft-fouth-
eaft. It appeared to me that weft-north-
weft of its entrance, towards Karagui, vef-
felf

fels may fafely anchor, and be fheltered from
the fouth, the weft, and the north winds:
The fouth of its entrance does not afford fo
good a harbour, as it is faid to have various
fand banks; I was obliged to truft to report, the ice and the fnow preventing me
from obtaining any better information.

We travelled this day feventy werfts, and
came in the evening to Karagui, which is
upon an eminence, and affords a view of
the fea. It has only three yourts and twelve
balagans, at the foot of which the river
Karaga paffes. This river pours itfelf into
the fea at the diftance of a few gun fhots
from the oftrog, which is the laft in the diftrict of Kamtfchatka; a hamlet a hundred
werfts farther, and containing but few
Kamtfchadales, not being included within
its limits,

As we were obliged to wait here for a
Q 3   ftock

ftock of dried fifh, not yet come up, and
intended for the nourifhment of our dogs in
the deferts, which we are now to traverfe, I
fhall embrace this opportunity of tranf-
cribing various notes made in this and the
preceding villages.   They will not be placed
in the fame order as they were written ; it
muft be fuppofed that the rapidity with
which we travelled, frequently left me no
choice in this refpect *.

I fhall firft fpeak of the yourts, which I
have not yet defcribed, deferving as they
are of particular attention.   Thefe ftrange
houfes are funk in the earth, as I before obferved, and the top, which appears above

---

* I fhall be cenfured perhaps for making my narrative
abound with dry and uniform details.   I would willingly
fpare the reader in this refpect, if I had not promifed to
obferve the utmoft accuracy.   Let him confider the objects
with which I am furrounded in the immenfe extent of
country that I travel, and he will perceive that they are
almoft always the fame.   Dces it then depend upon me to
vary my defcriptions, and avoid tautology ?

ground,

ground, is like a truncated cone. To
form a juft idea of them, we muft conceive
of a large fquare hole about twelve or fourteen yards in diameter, and eight feet deep ;
the four fides are lined with joifts or boards,
and the interftices of thefe walls are filled
up with earth, ftraw, or dried grafs, and
ftones. In the bottom of this hole various
pofts are fixed, that fupport the crofs beams
upon which the roof refts. The roof begins upon a level with the ground, and
rifes four feet above it ; it is two feet thick,
has a very gradual flope, and is made of the
fame materials as the walls. Towards the
top is a fquare opening, about four feet
long and three wide, which ferves as a paffage for the fmoke * and an entrance to the

* There is fuch a continual fmoke in thefe fubterraneous
habitations, that the opening in the roof is not fufficient to
let it out, and there is therefore in an unoccupied corner of
the yourt, behind the fire-place, a kind of vent-hole in an
oblique direction. It is called *joupann*; it terminates
without, at a little diftance from the fquare opening, and
is commonly clofed up with a mat or ftraw covering.

Q 4   yourt,

yourt, where the women as well as the
men go in and out by means of a ladder,
or notched beam, that is raifed to a level
with this opening. There is another very
low entrance in one fide of the yourt, but
it is confidered as a kind of difgrace to
make ufe of it. I fhall terminate the defcription of the exterior part of thefe habitations by adding, that they are furrounded
with tolerably high palifades, doubtlefs as
a protection againft the gales of wind, or
falls of fnow; it is faid, however, that thefe
enclofures formerly ferved as ramparts to
defend thefe people againft their enemies.

We have no fooner defcended thefe favage
abodes, than we wifh ourfelves out again;
the view and the fmell are equally offenfive.
The interior part confifts of one entire
room, about ten feet high. A bench, five
feet wide, and covered with various fkins,
half worn out, extends all round it. This
bench

bench is only a foot from the ground*, and commonly ferves as a bed for a number of families. I have counted in one yourt more than twenty perfons, men, women, and children. They eat, drink, and fleep pell mell together, fatisfy all the calls of nature without reftraint or modefty, and never complain of the noxious air that prevails in thefe places. It is true there is a fire almoft inceffantly. The fire-place is commonly either in the middle of the yourt or againft one of the fides. In the evening they rake the coals in a heap, and fhut the entrance of the yourt, where the fmoke fhould evaporate ; and thus the heat is concentrated, and kept up during the whole night. By means of a difmal lamp, the form and difagreeable fmell of which I have before defcribed, we difcover in one

* Some of the yourts which I faw were floored with planks ; but this is regarded as a luxury, and the generality have no other floor than the ground,

corner

corner of the apartment * a wretched image
of fome faint, fhining with greafe and
blackened with fmoke. It is before thefe
images that the Kamtfchadales bow themfelves, and offer their prayers. The reft of
the furniture confifts of feats and fome veffels, made either of wood, or the bark of
trees. Their cookery utenfils are of copper
or iron; but they are all difguftingly filthy.
The remains of their dried fifh are fcattered
about the room, and the women or the
children are continually broiling pieces of
falmon fkin, which is one of their favourite
meats.

The fingularity of the children's drefs
particularly attracted my attention; it is
faid exactly to refemble that of the Koriacs.
It confifts of only one garment, that is, of a

* This nook is in a manner diftinct from the room, and
is lefs filthy, becaufe it is lefs frequented. It is a place of
honour fet apart for ftrangers.

fingle deer fkin, that covers and fits clofe to every part of the body, fo that the children feem to be entirely fewed up. An opening at the bottom, before and behind, affords an opportunity of cleaning them. This opening is covered with another piece of fkin, which may be faftened and lifted up at pleafure ; it fupports a tuft of mofs *, placed like a clout between the legs of the child, and which is renewed as often as it becomes neceffary. Befides the common fleeves, there are two others hanging to the gar- ment to place the arms of the child in when it is cold ; the extremities are fewed up, and the fleeves lined on the infide with mofs. There is alfo a hood fitted to it, made of the fame materials as the reft of the drefs ; but in yourts the heads of the children are al- moft always bare, and the hood hangs there- fore upon their fhoulders. Befide all this,

* They make ufe of the herb called *tonnchitcha* for the fame purpofe.

they

they have a deer fkin girt, which ferves as a
fafh. The women carry their children on
their back by means of a ftring, which paffes
round the forehead of the mother and under
the buttocks of the child.

The toyon of Karagui, at whofe houfe we
lodged, was an old rebel. It was with fome
difficulty he had been brought back to his
duty, and he gave us fome uneafinefs by his
pofitive refufal to procure us fifh.

The manners of the inhabitants of this
oftrog are very fimilar to thofe of the neighbouring Koriacs. This analogy is as con-
fpicuous in their idiom as in the drefs of
their children. I had an opportunity of
remarking it the day after our arrival.

Underftanding that there were two hordes
of rein deer Koriacs at no great diftance,
we fent immediately a meffenger to them to
requeft

requeſt that they would ſell us ſome of
their animals. They readily complied, and
brought us the ſame day two rein deer
alive. This ſupply came very ſeaſonably
to the relief of our people, who began to
apprehend a want of proviſions. Meanwhile
our dogs were in ſtill greater danger of famine, as the dried fiſh was not yet arrived.
A rein deer was ordered to be killed directly; but when we were deſirous of knowing the price of it, we found very conſiderable difficulty in being able to treat with
the ſellers: they ſpoke neither Ruſſian nor
Kamtſchadale; and we ſhould never have
underſtood one another, if we had not fortunately met with an inhabitant of Karagui, who could ſerve as an interpreter.

There are two ſorts of Koriacs; thoſe
who are properly called by that name have
a fixed reſidence ; the others are wanderers,
and are known by the appellation of *rein*
deer

dœr Koriacs*. Their flocks are very numerous, and they maintain them by conducting
them to thofe cantons that abound with
mofs. When thefe paftures are exhaufted,
they feek for others. In this manner they
wander about inceffantly, encamping under
tents of fkin, and fupporting themfelves
with the produce of their deer.

Thefe animals are as ferviceable for
draught to the Koriacs, as the dogs are to
the Kamtfchadales. The perfons who came
to us were drawn by two rein deer. The
mode of harneffing and guiding them, as
as well as the form of the fledge, ought to
be defcribed ; but I think it better to defer
my defcription till I come to travel with
thefe people, as I fhall be able to be more
accurate.

* There are fome of thefe wandering Koriacs, I am
told, in the ifland of Karagui, which is twenty-fix werfts
from the village of that name. I had before imagined that
I could perceive this ifland at a diftance.

Our

Our long expected provifions arrived at laft on the evening of 29, and were brought by the fergeant whom we had waited for We prepared every thing for our departure the next morning, but a moft impetuous wind rofe in the night from the weft and the north-weft. This hurricane was accompanied with fnow, which fell in fuch abundance that we were obliged to prolong our ftay. Nothing fhort of this bad weather could have detained us. The arrival of our provifion had increafed our impatience; the fupply befide was not confiderable, and our neceffities were fo urgent that we were obliged to begin upon it immediately. It was therefore our intereft to be as expeditious as poffible, left our ftock fhould be confumed before we had paffed the deferts.

The wind abated in the courfe of the morning, but the fnow continued, and the fky

fky feemed to threaten us with a fecond
tempeft before the end of the day. It began to rife about two o'clock in the afternoon, and lafted till the evening.

To divert our attention, it was propofed
to us to try the abilities of a celebrated female dancer, who was a Kamtfchadale, and
lived in this oftrog. The encomiums beftowed upon her excited our curiofity, and
we fent for her; but either from caprice or
ill humour fhe refufed to dance, and paid
no regard to our invitation. It was in vain
they reprefented that her refufal was difref-
pectful to the governor general; no confideration could induce her to comply. Fortunately we had fome brandy by us, and a
bumper or two feemed to effect a change in
her inclinations. At the fame time Kamta-
fchadale, at our requeft, began to dance
before her, challenging her by his voice and
geftures. Gradually her eyes fparkled, her
coun-

countenance became convulfive, and her whole frame fhook upon the bench where fhe fat. To the enticements and fhrill fong of the dancer, fhe anfwered in fimilar accents, beating time with her head, which turned in every direction. The movements became at laft fo rapid, that, no longer able to contain herfelf, fhe darted from her feat, and in turn defied her man by cries and diftortions ftill more extravagant. It is not eafy to exprefs the abfurdity of the dance. All her limbs feemed to be disjointed; fhe moved them with equal ftrength and agility; fhe tore her cloaths, and fixed her hands to her bofom with a kind of rage as if fhe would tear it alfo. Thefe fingular tranfports were accompanied with ftill more fingular poftures; and in fhort, it was no longer a woman, but a fury. In her blind frenzy fhe would have rufhed into the fire that was kindled in the middle of the room, if her hufband had not taken the precau-

tion

tion of placing a bench before it to prevent her : during the whole dance indeed he took care to keep himfelf clofe to her. When he faw that her head was perfectly gone, that fhe ftaggered on all fides, and could no longer fupport herfelf without laying hold of her fellow dancer, he took her in his arms and placed her upon a bench, where fhe fell, like an inanimate clod, without confcioufnefs, and out of breath. She continued five minutes in this fituation. Meanwhile the Kamtfchadale, proud of his triumph, continued to dance and to fing. Recovering from her fwoon, the woman heard him, and fuddenly, in fpite of her weaknefs, fhe raifed herfelf up, uttered fome inarticulate founds, and would have begun again this labourous conteft. Her hufband kept her back, and interceded for her ; but the conqueror, believing himfelf to be indefatigable, continued his jeers and bantering, and we were obliged to exert our authority

to

to quiet him. In fpice of the praifes that
were lavifhed upon the talents of thefe ac-
tors, the fcene, I confefs, afforded me no
amufement, but on the contrary, confiderable difguft

All the inhabitants of this place, women
as well as men, fmoke and chew tobacco.
By a refinement that I cannot account for,
they mix afhes with the tobacco to make it
ftronger. We gave them fome fnuff, and
they applied it not to their nofe, but to their
mouth. I examined their pipes: they are
of the fame fhape as thofe of the Chinefe,
made of bone, and very fmall. When they
make ufe of them, they do not emit the
fmoke from their mouth, but fwallow it
with great gratification.

All the toyons of the different oftrogs we
had paffed in coming from Ozernoi, out of
refpect to M. Kafloff, had efcorted us as

far

far as Karagui. The fecond day after our
arrival, they had taken their leave of us to
return to their refpective habitations. Their
adieux were affectionate. After making
new apologies for not having been able to
give him a better reception in the courfe of
his journey, they fhowed the utmoft regret
at leaving him, as if he had been furrounded by the moft imminent dangers, and offered him whatever they poffeffed, ignorant
of any other way of teftifying their attachment. They addreffed themfelves in like
manner to me, and folicited me with ear-
neftnefs to receive fomething from them. It
was ufelefs to make objections ; my refufals
only rendered them the more urgent, and
to fatisfy them I was obliged to accept their
prefents.

Let me be permitted in this place to perform a duty which I owe to the Kamtfchadales

dales in general, for the civility with which they treated me. I have already mentioned their mild and hofpitable character, but I have not been fufficiently minute refpecting the inftances of regard which thefe good people gave me, and I recall with pleafure the rememberance of their kind reception. There was not, I believe, an individual chief of any oftrog, that did not make me fome trifling prefent. Sometimes it was a fable or fox fkin, and fometimes fruit or fifh, and fuch other objects as they conceived would be moft agreeable to me. One would have fuppofed that they had refolved, by their attentions to me, to repair the injuftice which they had fo long committed againft the French name. They often thanked me for having undeceived them upon the fubject; and fometimes again were tempted to regret it, when they confidered that they fhould fee me no more, and that it feldom

R 3 happened

happened that any of my countrymen vifited their peninfula.

We left Karagui at one o'clock in the morning of 2 March. The weather was tolerably calm, and continued fo during the whole day. The only inconvenience we met with, was the not being able to crofs, as we had hoped to do, a bay which the tempeft of the preceding evening had cleared of its ice: we were obliged to go round it. This bay has confiderable depth, is eight or ten werfts wide, and appeared to run in the direction of north-eaft and fouth-weft. The ice was only broken up- as far as the mouth, where it became folid again, and extended into the fea. With the circuit which we were obliged to make, we travelled this day about fifty werfts.

Upon the approach of night, we ftopped

in

in the open country and erected our tents.
Under the largeſt, belonging to M. Kaſloff,
were placed his vezock and mine, the door
of the one againſt the door of the other,
ſo that by letting down the windows, we
were able to converſe together. The other
ſledges were ranged two abreaſt round our
tents, and the ſpaces between, being covered with linen or ſkins, ſerved our guides
and our ſuite as places where they might
ſhelter themſelves, and prepare their beds.
Such was the diſpoſition of our halt.

As ſoon as our kettle boiled we took tea,
and then prepared for our ſupper, which
was our only meal every day. A corporal
preſided as *maitre d'hotel* and as cook. The
meats which weie prepared by him were
neither numerous nor delicate, but his
quickneſs and our appetites rendered us
indulgent. He commonly ſerved us up a
kind of ſoup made of a biſcuit of black bread,

and mixed with rice and oatmeal. It was prepared in half an hour, and in the following manner. He took a piece of beef, or flefh of rein deer, and put it into boiling water, having firft cut it into very thin flices, which were ready in an inftant.

The evening previous to our departure from Karagui, we had killed and begun upon our fecond deer. We regaled ourfelves with the marrow : raw or dreffed, I thought it excellent. We had the tongue alfo boiled, and I conceived that I had never eaten any thing more delicious.

We purfued our journey early in the morning, but it was impoffible to travel more than thirty-five werfts. The wind had changed to the weft and fouth-weft; it blew with extreme violence, and beat the fnow in our faces. Our guides fuffered extremely, lefs however than our dogs,

fome

fome of whom, exhaufted with fatigue, died on the road, and others were incapable of drawing us for want of nourifhment. We could only give them a fourth part of their common allowance, and had fcarcely enough left to laft two days.

In this extremity we difpatched a foldier to the oftrog of Kaminoi, to procure us fuccour, and to fend the efcort to meet us that was to have waited there till M. Kaf-loff arrived. It was a guard of forty-men, fent from Ingiga, upon the firft intelligence of the revolt of the Koriacs.

We were only fifteen werfts from the village or hamlet of Gavenki, where we hoped to find a fupply of fifh for our dogs ; and our confidence was fo great that we ventured to give them a double portion, that they might be the better able to con-vey us thither. Having paffed the night in the

the fame manner as the preceding, we purfued our journey at three o'clock in the
morning.   We quitted not the fea coaft
till we came to Gavenki, which was about
ten o'clock.   The name of the village is
derived from the word *gavna,* which fignifies excrement; and it is fo called on account of its deformity and wretched ftate.
There are in reality but two ifbas falling to
ruin, and fix balagans very ill conftructed
of bad and crooked wood, which the fea
leaves fometimes upon the fhore; for there
is not a tree in the whole neighbourhood,
and nothing to be feen but a few paltry
fhrubs fcattered here and there at a confiderable diftance from one another.   I was
not aftonifhed to learn, that not along ago,
more than twenty of the inhabitants voluntarily abandoned their country to feek out
a better abode.   At prefent the population
of this hamlet does not exceed five families,
including that of the toyon, and two Kamtfchadales

fchadales from the ifland of Karagui, who
are fettled there.   No reafon was affigned
for this removal, and I doubt whether they
have gained by the change.

We had not been an hour at Gavenki,
when a defpute arofe between a fergeant
of our company, and two peafants of the
village, to whom he had applied for wood.
They anfwered bluntly that they would not
give him any.   From one thing to another
the quarrel became violent.   The Kamtfchadales, little intimidated by the threats
of the fergeant, drew their knives * and
fell upon him; but they were immediately difarmed by two of our foldiers.
As foon as M. Kafloff was informed of this
violence,. he ordered that the guilty fhould
be punifhed as an example.   They were
brought before the yourt in which we were,

* Thefe knives are about two feet long ; they are worn
in their girdle, and hang upon the thigh.

and

and in order to awe the reft of the inhabitants, M. Kafloff went out himfelf to haften
the punifhment. I was left with the toyon,
who began to complain to me of the rigour
with which his two countrymen were treated. The family furrounded me and mur-
mured ftill louder. I was alone ; meanwhile I was endeavouring to pacify them,
when I perceived that the governor had
left his arms behind him. I haftily caught
up our fabres, upon a motion which the
toyon made to go out, and followed him.
He had already joined M. Kafloff, and ftir-
ring up all his neighbours, he demanded
in a high tone that the delinquents fhould
be releafed. He was himfelf, he faid, their
fole judge, and it belonged to him only to
punifh them. To thefe feditious clamours
M. Kafloff anfwered only by a ftern look,
which difconcerted the effrontery both of
the peafants and their chiefs. The toyon
ftill muttered fome words, but he was feized
and

and forced to affift in the chaftifement that he had been fo defirous of preventing. One of the culprits was a young man about eighteen years of age, and the other from twenty eight to thirty. They were ftripped and laid proftrate on the ground ; two foldiers held their hands and their feet, while four others beftowed upon their fhoulders a copious diftribution of lafhes. They were whipped in this manner one after another with rods of dried fir, till their bodies were covered with blood. At the entreaties of the women, whom the weaknefs of the fex renders every where compaffionate, the intended punifhment was leffened, and the young man given up to them. They immediately gave him a fine lecture on the folly of his conduct, which they might as well have fpared, as he was fcarcely in a fituation to attend to it, and ftill lefs to think of repeating his crime.

The

The feverety which M. Kafloff obferved
upon this occafion, was fo much the more
neceffary, as we began to perceive in this
village fome fymptoms of the contagious
turbulent difpofition of the Koriacs. Con-
trafted with the Kamtfchadales whom we
had juft quitted, the manners of the inhabitants of Gavenki led us to doubt whether it were really the fame people We
had as much reafon to complain of the
morofenefs and deceit of the latter, as we
had to boaft of the zeal and kindnefs of the
former. In fpite of all our importunities
we could get no provifion for our dogs.
They coldly informed us that they had
none; but their equivocal anfwers betrayed
them, and our people foon fatisfied themfelves of its falfehood. By means of our
dogs, whofe nofe and hunger were infallible
guides, they quickly difcovered the fubterraneous refervoirs, where the inhabitants
had, upon our approach, buried their provifions,

viſions, though the utmoſt care had been
taken to conceal all veſtiges of them, by
artfully covering them with earth and ſnow.
At the ſight of theſe caves, and the fiſh
that were drawn from them, theſe peaſants
began to allege the moſt paltry reaſons to
juſtify their conduct, and which only tended
to increaſe our indignation. We had ſome
ſentiments of humanity, or we ſhould have
taken their whole ſtock ; we contented
ourſelves with a ſmall part. From the nature of the proviſions it appeared that theſe
coaſts afforded them ſalmon, herring, cod,
morſe, and other amphibious animals.

There is neither ſpring nor river of any
ſort in the neighbourhood, but merely a
lake that ſupplies the inhabitants with water. In winter they break the ice that oc-
vers it, and carry home large pieces of it,
which they place in a trough ſuſpended in
the yourt about five or ſix feet high. The
heat

heat is fufficient to diffolve the ice; and to
this trough they have recourfe when they
are thirfty.

Near this village is a mountain or kind
of Kamtfchadale entrenchment, which formerly ferved them as a place of refuge when
they revolted.

We ftaid at Gavenki only twelve or thirteen hours. We fet off in the night for
Pouftaretfk, which is at the diftance of
more than two hundred werfts from it.
We were five days in travelling it, and no
journey had ever been fo painful. We
had no reafon to complain of the weather
during the firft day; but the next we were
extremely haraffed by the fnow and gales
of wind, which fucceeded without interruption, and with fuch impetuofity that
our conductors were blinded. They could
diftinguifh no object four paces from them,
and

and could not even fee the fledge that immediately followed them.

To increafe our misfortune, our Gavenki guide was old and fhort fighted, and frequently therefore went out of the road. We were then obliged to ftop while he went on before to find the veftiges of the road; but how was it poffible to find them in fo extenfive a plain, covered with fnow, and where we could perceive neither tree, nor mountain, nor river? The experience of our guide was continually at fault from the badnefs of the weather, notwithftanding the incredible knowledge he had of thefe roads. The fmalleft rifing, the leaft fhrub, was fufficient to fet him right; meanwhile we calculated that the deviations he occafioned us amounted each day to twenty werfts.

At the end of the fecond day's journey,

my

my dogs were reduced to a fingle fifh,
which I divided between them. The want
of food foon exhaufted their ftrength, fo as
to make them unable to proceed. Some
fell under the blows of our conductors,
others refufed to draw, and many from in-
anition died on the fpot. Of the thirty-
feven dogs that were harneffed to my vezock upon leaving Bolcheretfk, only twenty-
three remained, and thefe were reduced to
the utmoft poverty. M. Kafloff had in like
manner loft a confiderable number of his.

The famine became at laft fo great, that
we were apprehenfive of being ftarved to
death in this defert. Not having a morfel
of fifh left for our dogs, we were obliged to
feed them with part of our own provifions ;
but their fhare was very moderate, prudence requiring us to obferve the moft rigid
œconomy.

In

In this woeful conjuncture, we left our
equipage in the midſt of the way, under
guard of ſome of our conductors, and having choſen the moſt tolerable of the dogs
to ſupply the place of thoſe which we had
loſt, we went on.

Our pain and anxiety continued. We
were in want of water. The only little
brook that we found was entirely frozen up,
and we were obliged to quench our thirſt
with the ſnow. The want of wood was
another difficulty. Not a tree had we ſeen
during the whole journey, and we frequently went a werſt out of our way, perhaps for a paltry ſhrub not a foot long.
We gathered all that we ſaw, for fear of
finding none as we proceeded farther ; but
they were ſo ſmall and ſo few as not to
enable us to cook our victuals. To warm
ourſelves was out of the queſtion. In the
mean time the cold was extremely rigorous,

and

and from the flow pace that we travelled, we were nearly frozen. Almoſt at every inſtant we were alſo under the neceſſity of ſtopping to unharneſs the dogs, that expired one after another.

I cannot deſcribe what my feelings were in this ſituation. My mind ſuffered ſtill more than my body. The inconveniences that were common to us, I patiently ſhared with my companions ; their example and my youth gave me courage to ſupport them. But when I thought of my diſpatches, my conſtancy forſook me. They were continually in my hands, and I never touched them without ſhuddering. My anxiety to execute my truſt, the view of the many obſtacles I had to ſurmount, the uncertainty of ſucceeding, all theſe ideas united to torment me. I endeavoured to diſpel them; a moment after ſome new obſtacle brought them to my mind with additional force.

Upon

Upon leaving Gavenki, we had quitted
the eaſtern coaſt, and the weſtern preſented itſelf to our view two werſts from Pou-
ſteretſk. We had croſſed therefore the
whole width of this part of Kamtſchatka,
which is not leſs than two hundred werſts,
or fifty leagues. We travelled this extent of country more on foot than in our
ſledges. Our dogs were ſo weak, that we
were willing to fatigue ourſelves in order
to relieve them, but they were ſeldom the
more alert on this account. Our conductors could not make them go on without
harneſſing themſelves in like manner to the
ſledge, and thus aſſiſt them to draw us along ;
we encouraged them alſo by ſhowing them
a handkerchief folded up in the ſhape of a
fiſh. They followed this bait, which diſ-
appeared the moment they approached near
enough to lay hold of it.

It was by theſe contrivances that we were
able

able to paſs the mountain that leads to
Pouſtaretſk. From the civil manner in
which the women received us, I conſidered
myſelf as ſafe the moment I ſet foot in this
hamlet. Six of them came to meet us, ex-
hibiting the moſt abſurd demonſtrations of
joy. We underſtood, from ſome words
they ſpoke, that their huſbands were gone
to the oſtrog of Potkagornoï in purſuit of
whales. They conducted us to their habitations, ſinging and ſkipping about us like
ſo many maniacs. One of them took off
her parque, made of the ſkin of a young
deer, and put it upon M. Kaſloff; the reſt
by loud burſts of laughter expreſſed their
ſatisfaction at our arrival, which they ſaid
was unexpected. This was ſcarcely probable, but we pretended to believe them,
in hopes of meeting with the better fare.

We entered Pouſtaretſk 9 March, at
three o'clock in the afternoon. Our firſt
                                precaution

precaution was to vifit all the refervoirs of
fifh. How great was our mortification to
find them empty! We immediately fufpected that the inhabitants had acted in
the fame manner as thofe of Gavenki ; and
we queftioned the women, and ranfacked
every probable place, perfuaded that they
had concealed their provifions. The more
they denied it, the farther we purfued
our refearches. They were however fruitlefs, and we could find nothing.

During this interval our dogs had been
unharneffed in order to be tied up in troops
as ufual. They were no fooner faftened to
the pofts, than they fell upon their ftrings
and their harneffes, and devoured them in
a moment. It was in vain that we attempted to retain them ; the majority efcaped
into the country, and wandered about con-
fuming whatever their teeth could penetrate. Some died, and became immediately

S 4 the

the prey of the reſt. They ruſhed with
eagerneſs upon the dead carcaſſes, and tore
them to pieces. Every limb that any individual ſeized upon, was conteſted by a troop
of competitors, who attacked it with equal
avidity: if he fell under their numbers, he
became in turn the objeȼt of a new combat*.
To the horror of ſeeing them devour one
another, ſucceeded the melancholy ſpeȼta-
cle of thoſe that beſet our yourt. The
leanneſs of theſe poor beaſts was truly
affeȼting: they could ſcarcely ſtand upon
their legs. By their plaintive and inceſſant
cries, they ſeemed to addreſs themſelves to
our compaſſion, and to reproach our inca-
pacity to relieve them. Many of them,
who ſuffered as much from cold as from
hunger, laid themſelves down by the opening made in the roof of the yourt to let

* To guard ourſelves againſt theſe famiſhed dogs we
never dared to go out without our ſticks, or ſome kind of
arms to drive them off.

out

out the fmoke. The more they felt the benefit of the heat, the nearer they approached ; and at laft, either from faintnefs, or ina-
bility to preferve an equiliribum, they fell
into the fire before our eyes.

Shortly after our arrival the guide returned, who had accompanied the foldier
fent out fix days before to Kaminoi to procure us fuccour. He informed us that our
meffenger was reduced to the laft extremity,
and confidered himfelf as fortunate in having found, twelve werfts to the north of
Poufteretfk, a miferable deferted yourt,
where he had fheltered himfelf from the
tempefts, which had mifled him no lefs than
ten times. The provifion we had given him
for himfelf and his dogs was all confumed,
and he waited impatiently till he fhould be
relieved from his embaraffment, without
which it was impoffible for him to come out
of his afylum, either for the purpofe of
executing

executing his commiffion, or of returning back to us.

M. Kafloff, far from being caft down by this new difappointment, animated our courage by communicating to us the laft expedients he had refolved to employ. He had already, upon the intelligence of a whale being driven on fhore near Potkagornoï, difpatched an exprefs to that village. The utmoft expedition was recommended, and he was to bring as much of the flefh and fat of the whale as he could. This refource however being uncertain, M. Kafloff propofed that we fhould facrifice the fmall quantity of provifion which each of us had intended to referve for the fupport of his own dogs. This contribution was for fergeant Kabechoff, who had offered to go to Kaminoi. In the diftrefs in which we were, the moft feeble ray of hope was fufficient to induce us to rifk our all. We embraced therefore

therefore the propofal with tranfport, con-
fiding in the zeal and ability of this fergeant.

He departed the 10, minutely inftructed
upon the fubject of his journey, and carrying with him the whole of our provifions. In
his way he was to take up our poor foldier,
and from thence proceed to fulfil the commiffion in which he had failed. Having
taken all thefe precautions, we exhorted one
another to patience, and endeavoured to
divert our anxiety by waiting till it fhould
pleafe providence to deliver us. I fhall employ this time in giving an account of the
obfervations I made at Pouftaretfk.

This hamlet is fituated upon the declivity
of a mountain wafhed by the fea ; for we
cannot call a river*, what is nothing more

* It is called by the people of this country *Pouftaïa-*
reka, or defert river. This gulf was entirely frozen over.

than

than a very narrow gulf, which reaches as
far as the foot of this mountain. The water is falt, and not drinkable; we were obliged therefore to have recourfe to melted
fnow, which was the only frefh water we
could procure. Two yourts, inhabited by
about fifteen perfons, make up the whole
hamlet. I mean to include a few balagans
that are occupied in fummer, and fituated
farther from the fhore.

They fpend the whole fummer in fifhing,
and preparing their ftock of winter provifions. If we may judge from the food that
we faw them drefs and eat, this part of the
country does not much abound with fifh.
Their aliment during our refidence among
them confifted only in the flefh and fat of
the whale, the bark of trees in its natural
ftate, and in buds fteeped in the oil of the
whale, or the fea wolf, or in the fat of any
other animal. They informed us that they
                                        fre-

frequently caught fmall cod in the open fea;
I know not whether they had any concealed
ftore of this article, but we had fearched
fo thoroughly, and we faw them fare fo
wretchedly, that we believed them to be
really as poor as they appeared to be.

Their mode of catching rein deer, which
are very plentiful in thefe cantons, is e-
qually fure and eafy. They furround a
certain extent of land with palifades, leaving here and there an opening, where they
fpread their nets or fnares. They then
difperfe, in order to drive the deer into
them. Thefe animals, by attempting to
fave themfelves, run through the openings,
and are caught either by the neck or their
horns. A confiderable number always efcape by tearing the nets or leaping the palifades; meanwhile twenty or thirty men
will frequently take at a time upwards of
fixty deer.

Independ-

Independently of their domeſtic occupations, the women are employed in preparing, ſtaining, and ſewing the ſkins of various animals, particularly deer ſkins. They
firſt ſcrape them with a ſharp ſtone fixed in
a ſtick. Having taken off the fat, they ſtill
continue to ſcrape them to make them
thinner and more ſupple. The only colour they ſtain them is a deep red, which
is extracted from the bark of a tree called
in Ruſſia *olkhovaïa-dereva*, and known to us
by the name of *alder*. They boil the bark,
and then rub the ſkin with it till it has imbibed the die. The knives which they afterwards make uſe of to cut theſe ſkins, are
crooked, and the invention probably of the
country.

The ſinews of the rein deer ſtripped very
ſlender, and prepared in like manner by
the women, ſerves them inſtead of thread.
They ſew perfectly well. Their needles,
which

which have nothing fingular, are brought from Okotfk, and their thimbles are like thofe ufed by our tailors, and are always worn upon the fore-finger.

I have already given an account of their manner of fmoking, but I muft refume the fubject, in order to relate the fatal confequences that attend it. Their pipes* will fcarcely contain more than a pinch of tobacco, which they renew till they have fatiated themfelves ; and this is effected in the following manner. By fwallowing the fmoak, inftead of blowing it out, they gradually become fo intoxicated that they would, if they were near it, fall into the fire. Experience has happily taught them to attend to the progrefs of this fpecies of trance,

---

* The tubes of thefe pipes are made of wood, with a flit from one end to the other. Thus they open in the middle, and the fmoakers, from œconomy, fcrape the infide after ufing, and make a fecond regale of the filings.

and

and they have the precaution to fit down or to lay hold of the firft object within their reach. The fit lafts them at leaft for a quarter of an hour, during which time their fituation is the moft painful that can be conceived. Their bodies are covered with a cold perfpiration, the faliva diftils from their lips, their breathing is fhort, and attended with a conftant inclination to cough. It is only when they have brought themfelves into this fituation, that they conceive themfelves to have enjoyed the true pleafure of fmoking.

Neither the men nor the women wear chemifes*; their common garment has nearly the fame form, but it is fhorter, and made of deer fkin. When they go out, they put on a warmer one over it. In

---

* In defcribing the drefs of the Kamtfchadales, we obferved that they wore under their parque a fmall chemife made of nankin, or cotton ftuff.

winter

winter the women wear fur breeches inftead of petticoats.

The 12, M. Schmaleff joined us. His
return gave us the greater pleafure, as we
had been very uneafy on his account. He
had been abfent from us fix weeks, and
almoft a month had elapfed fince the time
fixed for his meeting us. He had very little
provifion left, but his dogs were not in fo
bad a condition as ours, and we embraced
the opportunity of fetching our equipage
which we had left in the road, and of which
we had not fince received any news.

The fouth-weft wind, which had fo much
incommoded us in our journey, continued
to blow with equal violence for feveral days;
it afterwards changed to the north-eaft, but
the weather only became the more terrible.

It feemed as if nature in anger confpired

VOL. I. T alfo

alfo againft us to increafe our difficulties and prolong our mifery. I appeal to every man who has found himfelf in a fimilar fituation. He only can tell how cruel it is to be thus chained down by obftacles that are inceffantly fpringing up. We may ftrive to divert our thoughts, to arm ourfelves with patience ; our ftrength will at laft fail, and reafon lofe its power over us. Nothing renders a calamity more infupportable, than the not being able to forefee when it will terminate.

We had too painful an experience of this upon the receipt of the letters that were brought us from Kaminoi. We had no fuccour to expect from that quarter, Kabechoff informed us. The detachment from Ingiga were unable to come to us. They had been two months at Kaminoi, and had confumed not only their own ftock of provifion, but alfo the fupply that had been deftined

deftined for us. Their dogs, like ours, devoured one another, and the forty men were
reduced to the laft extremity. Our fergeant
added, that he had fent immediately to Ingiga as our only refource, and that he expected an anfwer in a few days; but he
feared that it would not be very fatisfactory, as the town muft be badly ftocked
with dogs and provifions, after the confiderable fupply which it had furnifhed.

This melancholy news deprived us of all
hope, and we gave ourfelves up for loft.
Our grief and defpondence were fo extreme,
that M. Kafloff was at firft infenfible to the
news of his promotion, which he had received by the fame meffenger. A letter
from Irkoutfk informed him, that, out of
gratitude for his fervices, the emprefs had
advanced him from the government of
Okotfk to that of Yakoutfk. In any other
fituation this news would have afforded him

T 2   the

the utmoſt pleaſure. A more extenſive field was open for the diſplay of his zeal, and a better opportunity for exerciſing his talents in the art of government. But his thoughts were very differently employed than in calculating the advantages of this new poſt. Every other ſentiment yielded to that of our danger, in which he was wholly abſorbed.

In a moment thus critical, I can only aſcribe to the inſpiration of heaven, the idea that ſuddenly occurred to me of ſeparating myſelf from M. Kafloff. In reflecting upon it, I perceived every thing there was in it diſobliging to him, and mortifying to me. I endeavoured to drive the idea from my mind, but it was in vain. It returned, it fixed itſelf there in ſpite of me. I thought of my country, of my family, of my duty. Their power over me was invincible, and I diſcloſed myſelf to the governor. Upon the
firſt

firſt view it appeared to him to be a wild projeĉt, and he failed not to oppoſe it. The deſire of executing it, furniſhed me with a ready anſwer to all his objeĉtions. I proved to him, that by continuing together, we deprived each other of the means of purſuing his journey. We could not ſet off together without a ſtrong reinforcement of dogs. We had ſcarcely more than twentyſeven that were at all tolerable, the reſt having died or being unfit for ſervice*. By giving up theſe twenty-ſeven dogs, one of us would be able to proceed, and his departure would relieve the other from the difficulty of maintaining this ſmall number of famiſhed ſteeds. But, ſaid M Kaſloff, you muſt ſtill have proviſion for them, and what means are there of procuring it?

I was at a loſs how to reply, when we were

---

* The reader will recolleĉt that upon leaving Bolcheretſk, we had a troop conſiſting nearly of three hundred.

informed

informed that our exprefs from Potkagornoï was arrived. More fortunate than the
reft, he had brought us a large quantity of
the flefh and fat of the whale. My joy at
the fight of it was extreme, every difficulty
was now removed, and I conceived myfelf
already to be out of Pouftaretfk. I returned
inftantly to my argument, and M. Kafloff,
having no longer any thing to oppofe, and
applauding in reality my zeal, complied
with my folicitations. It was fixed that I
fhould depart the 18 at lateft. From this
moment we were employed in the neceffary
arrangements for executing my projeǎ with
the greateft fafety.

Every thing flattered me with the hope
of fuccefs. With the melancholy news we had
received from Kaminoi, there were fome con-
foling circumftances. For inftance, we were
affured that no obftruǎion was to be appre-
hended from the Koriacs. A perfeǎ calm
was

was reeftablifhed among them ; and, to con-
vince us of it, they had been defirous that
fome of their countrymen fhould accompany
the foldier charged with the difpatches to
M. Kafloff. Even the fon of the chief of
the rebels, called *Eitel,* was one of the
efcort. The Koriacs, he told us, had long
waited with impatience the arrival of the
governor, and his father meant to fhow
his refpect to M. Kafloff by coming to meet
him.

Charmed with the idea that we had no
longer any thing to fear, at leaft on this
fide, we were eager to exprefs our fatisfaction to thefe Koriacs for their good will to
us. We made them all the prefents that
our fituation would permit, fuch as tobacco,
ftuffs, and various articles which I had purchafed during my fea voyage, as well as
others that had been left me by count de la
Peroufe. We gave them fomething alfo
for

for their relations. But our principal care was to make them as drunk as poffible, that they might give a favourable report of their reception. It was neceffary to confult their tafte; and to intoxicate them completely, they confidered as the very effence of politenefs.

I propofed to thefe Koriacs to take charge of two of my portmanteaus. They expreffed at firft fome unwillingnefs, on account of the diftance, which was as far as Ingiga. By means, however, of entreaties and my purfe, I at laft prevailed upon them to take them into their fledges. Eafed in this manner of my baggage, I had nothing to think of but my difpatches. The effects which I had intrufted to the Koriacs gave me little or no concern, as the foldier fent from Ingiga would return with them, and had promifed to fee that the truft was faithfully executed.

To

To the laſt moment of my ſtay M. Kafloff had been laboriouſly * employed in preparing his letters, which I was to have the care of. With theſe he delivered to me a *podarojenei*, or paſſport, that was to ſerve me as far as Irkoutſk. This paſſport was alſo an order to all Ruſſian officers and other inhabitants, ſubjects of the empreſs, whom I ſhould meet in my way to that place, to aſſiſt me with the means of proceeding on my journey with ſafety and expedition. The foreſight of the governor omitted nothing that was neceſſary for me. Had I been the brother of his heart, his attentions could not have been greater.

I muſt pauſe; for I cannot ſuppreſs the emotion I feel at the thought that I am upon the point of quitting this eſtimable

---

* It was really a labour, and a moſt fatiguing one, if we conſider that in theſe yourts it was not poſſible to write, without lying upon the ground; we were alſo ſuffocated with ſmoke, and the ink froze by our ſide.

man,

man, rendered for ever dear to me, ftill more
by the virtues of his heart than the accomplifhments of his underftanding. The ge-
nerous facrifice he made is at this moment
a weight upon me, and I cannot avoid re-
proaching myfelf for having wifhed it.
What do I not fuffer upon leaving him in
thefe frightful deferts, without knowing
whether he will ever be able to come out of
them! The image of his melancholy fituation haunts and agitates my mind. Ah! I
repeat it; it muft have been the convi&tion
that there was no other way of executing
the truft repofed in me, which impelled me,
in fpite of the prohibition of count de la
Peroufe, to take this refolution. But for
this motive, but for my difpatches, I could
never juftify to my own heart my eagernefs to leave him. May the teftimony
which my gratitude will ever render for his
goodnefs to me, and his zeal for the fervice
of his miftrefs, contribute in fome meafure

to

to his advancement and his happineſs! mine will be complete, if I have ever the pleaſure of feeing him again, and embracing him in my arms.

END OF THE FIRST VOLUME.

For EU product safety concerns, contact us at Calle de José Abascal, 56–1°, 28003 Madrid, Spain or eugpsr@cambridge.org.